...ights into
Troubled Sexuality

PSYCHOSEXUAL MEDICINE SERIES
Edited by Ruth L. Skrine MB, ChB, MRCGP

Psychosexual Medicine is a discipline which uses a combined body and mind approach to problems related to sexuality, and which stresses the importance of the doctor-patient relationship. The method derives from psychoanalysis but is distinct in that the practitioner listens to unconscious material over a focused narrow field. The work of many doctors and nurses and of some physiotherapists, provides opportunities for physical examination and treatment of the genital area which are unavailable to non-medical sexual therapists. Both physical and psychological problems and the interaction between them can be explored at the time of physical examination.

This series forms part of the developing body of knowledge held by members of the Institute of Psychosexual Medicine, formed in London in 1974. The books are for doctors and their colleagues who are interested in a psychosomatic approach to sexual problems particularly those working in general practice and gynaecology, as well as psychological and genito-urinary medicine.

Other titles in this series

Psychosexual Training and the Doctor/Patient Relationship
Edited by R. L. Skrine

Introduction to Psychosexual Medicine
Edited by R. L. Skrine

Psychosexual Medicine
A study of underlying themes
Edited by Rosemarie Lincoln

Insights into Troubled Sexuality
A case profile anthology

Revised edition

Prudence Tunnadine
Scientific Director, Institute of
Psychosexual Medicine, London

CHAPMAN & HALL
London · New York · Tokyo · Melbourne · Madras

Published by Chapman & Hall, 2–6 Boundary Row, London SE1 8HN

Chapman & Hall, 2–6 Boundary Row, London SE1 8HN, UK

Chapman & Hall, 29 West 35th Street, New York NY10001, USA

Chapman & Hall Japan, Thomson Publishing Japan, Hirakawacho Nemoto Building, 7F, 1-7-11 Hirakawa-cho, Chiyoda-ku, Tokyo 102, Japan

Chapman & Hall Australia, Thomas Nelson Australia, 102 Dodds Street, South Melbourne, Victoria 3205, Australia

Chapman & Hall India, R. Seshadri, 32 Second Main Road, CIT East, Madras 600 035, India

First published as *The Making of Love*
First edition 1983
Revised edition 1992

© 1983 Prudence Tunnadine
© 1992 Chapman & Hall

Typeset in 9½/11 Palatino by Mews Photosetting, Beckenham, Kent
Printed in Great Britain by Page Bros, Norwich

ISBN 0 412 43580 2

A catalogue record for this book is available from the British Library

Library of Congress Cataloging-in-Publication data available

Contents

Acknowledgements

This book is not about sexual performance. It is about people who for one reason or another have at some time in their lives not been able to enjoy their own sexuality, and who have sought help to do so. The people I describe are real, and the greatest problem has been how to protect the confidential relationship between doctor and patients. It is inevitable that some of my own patients may think they can recognize their story, and feel that their confidence has been betrayed. To do so would indeed be a betrayal, not only of that trust, but of my own sense of the privilege it is to spend my working life hearing and sharing the most private feelings of people about this aspect of their lives.

How then can I reassure them? Every identifiable detail which is not fundamentally relevant to the meaning of the problem has been changed: names, places, jobs. Details of conversation have been confined to those I have heard often. Nor are these the only possible examples of similar stories, though I have tried to avoid generalization. I have made composites, distillates, stereotypes perhaps. Although not all my own patients have sexual difficulty, most coming to see me simply about minor gynaecological matters, routine checks or family planning, I have had thousands of consultations during more than 30 years in this work. And while the conclusions I draw, the sometimes provocative kites that I fly, are mine alone, I have also heard accounts of patients in training and research seminars from hundreds of other doctors with comparable experience. Thus the people I describe, not always patients of my own, are representatives of a total clinical experience that would take a better mathematician than I to calculate. Nor would I if I could. It is of the essence of my philosophy and of this work that statistical head-counting, generalizing about variable individuals and labelling personal attitudes and behaviour is always and by definition false. I hold that the one certain fact about human beings is that each is unique; that no two people are ever quite the same as each other, and that no one person remains quite the same through life, or even from moment to moment.

To my patients, then, who are perhaps more likely to read · a book with my name on than are others, I say this. If you believe you recognize something of your story, you may know first that no-one else can do so, and secondly that it would not have been included had I not met and heard of many others — not identical for you are unique — but like you. Further, there will be many others whom my colleagues in the Institute of Psychosexual Medicine have treated who will be thinking the same — and their names and details have always been similarly changed, even in confidential professional discussion.

I hope, too, that if I have conveyed what I want to convey, thousands of others who have never met such doctors — any doctors — will be thinking, 'She's talking about me', — and that they will realize they are not alone.

A number of people have read parts or all of this book in preparation, and all have contributed encouragement and constructive criticism from their personal standpoint. Liz Calder and Faith Evans at Cape were patient and positive; my trust in Ruth Skrine, the late Jimmy Matthews and Rosemary Morris at Chapman & Hall to do what they would with this new edition seems to me to have proved fully justified. Celia Pridell in typing the manuscript while coping with her young family, found time to make useful comments from first to last. A few close friends did too, notably Tom Main and Nancy Raphael. My immediate family, of three generations and a rich variety of vocations, cope well with having a daughter, sister, mother working in a field which needs forever explaining, not to say explaining away. They all helped, and I thank them all — most of all for being who they are — with my love.

Dr Tom Main, psychoanalyst and past President of the Institute of Psychosexual Medicine, opened my eyes, as well as those of many of my colleagues, by being prepared to keep his own eyes open in his work with us over many years. If I could sum up the richness of his training and of our clinical experience and research in a few words, it would be his insistence never to think that we *know*; always to ask ourselves, 'What is going on here, now, in the present moment, with this one troubled person in front of me?' I thank him with respect for a distinguished master; with gratitude (and exasperation) for a colleague who expected us ever to do better; and with love for a dear friend.

I thank too all my other colleagues in the Institute for their contributions to my education and clinical experience. I cannot separate my own knowledge from theirs in the contents of this book.

I dedicate it to my patients; to all our patients. Ultimately we learn only from them , if we are open enough to do so.

Introduction

In the mid-1950s a group of doctors working in Family Planning Clinics had noticed that many women who were unhappy with the quality of their sexual lives chose, not always verbally or even consciously, to seek help when coming ostensibly for family planning advice. Contraception is after all by definition about purposes other than intercourse for procreation alone, and patients may reasonably expect a doctor offering such advice to be concerned with sex for pleasure.

These doctors, women with sexual and family lives of their own as well as specialized training in contraceptive gynaecology, aimed to diminish anxiety by giving advice and encouragement from their own knowledge and experience. It would be another 12 years before the behavioural advice programme of the Americans Masters and Johnson was to be published, but the principles behind our doctors' thinking at that time were not fundamentally different from theirs which we heard later, and which were to be received by many would-be therapists throughout the world as guidelines. We should not be surprised at this, for their experiments seemed to offer certainty in an area in which uncertainty and confusion is deeply threatening for patients and doctors alike.

Our doctors had had no formal sexual or psychotherapeutic training in their medical education; this is rare and patchy even today. They found their approach helped some patients but not all. Dissatisfied with their techniques, they asked Dr Michael Balint [1], a psychoanalyst interested in the application of psychoanalytic insight to everyday doctoring, to meet with them in a training-research seminar to study their work with such patients.

When this came to an end, Dr Tom Main, another distinguished psychoanalyst, decided that the group's findings were too interesting to abandon. He started another group under the auspices of the Family Planning Association, with the financial backing of Nancy Raphael and the Lord and Lady Monckton Fund, who have continued to support our work to this day. I joined the group in 1960, almost by accident. I remember thinking at my first visit that it seemed a bit 'psychological' for my taste, and thought merely that it would give me the excuse for a day out in London! Few of us then would have dreamed how absorbing our studies would become, or that from these modest beginnings would grow the nationwide organization of which I am Scientific Director, and which we call today the Institute of Psychosexual Medicine [2].

Hundreds of doctors have undertaken this training to date: family planning and family doctors, venereologists and gynaecologists, even a few psychiatrists. Most seek simply to understand and treat the patients who bring them their psychosexual or related psychosomatic or stress symptoms in the course of their normal work. From among them, however, a large number have proceeded to the level of specialization at which they come before an examining panel. If successful, they are awarded a certificate of competence by the Institute, which indicates that their skills are sufficient to deal with referrals from other consultants and agencies. Foreseeing that the demand for such training would fast outstrip the number of available psychoanalysts with group experience, Dr Main supervised a workshop at which some of these specialized doctors could acquire leadership techniques in order to train new groups of doctors in their own localities. The Institute appoints trained seminar leaders in most areas of the British Isles given enough interested doctors to make a viable group (and one in Australia), despite the traditional belief that only fully qualified psychoanalysts could manage such groups.

The training reflects the treatment method we have developed, in that it aims to encourage awareness and skill rather than to impart factual knowledge; it is concerned with identifying individual anxieties and blind spots rather than with theories of normality. Like any practical skill — surgery, golf, cooking — it cannot easily be defined. Ultimately in all these the individual, having read the books and attended the lectures, must try out and modify his own approach, whether to the exploratory operation, the swing which led to the bunker, or the sauce too garlicky for the family's taste. Doctors are trained to acknowledge their own prejudices and not to inflict them upon their patients, so as to free their patients to become aware of their own unique anxieties and to develop and trust their own sexual instincts and talents.

Formal medical education tends to discourage doctors from awareness of their own emotions. The aim, on the whole, is to overcome them or to hide them in 'objectivity' whenever possible. In this work, however, we learn to value such feelings and to develop a conscious awareness that different patients evoke them in us differently. If we can become sufficiently conscious of our own feelings, we can then observe the patient's contribution to our response as a useful clinical fact. We may wonder on their behalf whether this throws any light upon their difficulties in dealing with others in their lives, or upon their views of their own sexuality. In applying such psychoanalytic insight to the emotional content of the brief commonplace medical consultation, we may come to share with the patient ideas they are unable to recognize for themselves, and which have been interfering with their confidence sexually.

I shall elaborate on how this applies in practice by accounts of individual case profiles, but before leaving the history of the development of our work I must attempt to define the fundamental difference between this 'analytical' approach and the 'behavioural' method which guides couples through a structured programme of sexual technique. There is in this field plenty of work for us all, and it may be argued that in sexual matters the difference in aim is not important — whatever works will do. If we think further, however, as to whether we use our psychological techniques to help individuals find what is right for them, or rather to help them conform to our, or society's, view of a norm, it seems to me that the distinction between the two schools of thought is inescapable, and poses disturbing questions.

In the event, when Masters and Johnson's [3,4], and later Helen Singer Kaplan's [5] books arrived in Britain, we who already had 12 years of our own research and experience behind us could greet their ideas not with unquestioning surprise, but rather with objective criticism as to whether they threw light on or confirmed our own established findings. That their prohibitions on ambitious performance goals were designed to reduce the fear of failure made sense to us. So did the idea of reopening broken-down physical communication by an authority ordering touch and play at regular intervals. We had long known, however, that in a broadly literate society, not all patients need instructions about their sexual lives, and that examining with an individual why they had been unable to enjoy themselves was sometimes more effective — certainly quicker — than merely taking their plea of ignorance at face value and responding with our own bright ideas. Too often, we found, patients whom we had instructed continued to use us as the source of knowlege. They followed our instructions obediently to the letter and achieved in mechanical terms the desired sexual effect; their muscles in orgasm contracting at the rate per second we were now told was 'right', but they failed to 'own' their desires.

I shall elaborate also, in context, my disgreement with Masters and Johnson's assumptions about the nature of female orgasm. I wish here only to insist that in relation to their laboratory experiments, we were like the proverbial Irishman who, asked by the lost motorist the way to Cork, replied, 'I wouldn't start from here'. We were studying failures of personal confidence — something completely different from the measurement of anatomy and physiology in couples so confident and 'normal' as to be able to make love to order, in a laboratory, observed, and wired up to recording apparatus.

Will our studies prove to have made any positively fundamental breakthrough in the application of psychoanalysis? Only history will show, and I am too close to it to judge. Yet I believe it is possible that they have, and if so it will be found that the practice of medicine, in which doctors examine their patients' genitalia, can be used to achieve and to impart psychoanalytic insight.

It is widely held that psychoanalysis is essentially a non-touching discipline, and that to touch is to risk sexualizing the transference. The notion that genital examination can be employed without this taking place, and that the potentially sexual content of such an encounter can be calmly analysed and used fruitfully to convey new insights to the patient, will certainly shock and even horrify many traditional analysts. Yet this is our experience.

Arguably, then, the historical developments from Freud's beginnings by Jung and Adler and Ferenzy and the rest may be seen as variations on a theme. After Ferenzy, Michael and Enid Balint realized that psychoanalytic insight need not be confined to the couch but could be found and used in everyday, face-to-face medicine. Melanie Klein noticed that verbal techniques were useless to children and developed other methods of communication in allowing them the freedom of play, and making observations about that. Michael Balint's first 'Virgin Wives' [6] group noticed that interesting observations could be made at the moment of vaginal examination, and it is due to Tom Main's insistence with us 'ordinary' body doctors that we examine our feelings in these tricky and potentially sexual trans-actions that we stand back and think, and think again, that our knowledge was furthered. No-one who has trained with us doubts that it can be achieved. How far it can be developed to embrace all pyschosomatic medicine in the future remains to be seen.

I hope in this book to show, if I show nothing else, that people vary, and to convey the strong belief of the Institute of Psychosexual Medicine that it is always the person, rather than the anatomical parts of the performance, that counts. We have found that when people bring their sexual pro-blems to doctors, from whom they hope for emotional understanding as well as bodily care, their problems are rarely purely physical, rarely purely psychological, and almost never due to ignorance alone. The problems we meet are usually caused by the effect of tension or anxiety, not always fully conscious, upon bodily and emotional desires.

The case profile approach of the book is set in the con-text of the common problems that arise at different stages of life. Many of the profiles are drawn from several decades of work but doctors practising psychosexual medicine find that more sexually liberated generations still encounter many of the same problems.

The original edition of *The Making of Love* was aimed at the general public. This revised edition has been produced in response to the many requests from doctors who have found the book helpful in their professional work. It is intended for doctors in training seminars and working towards the certificate awarded by the Institute of Psycho-sexual Medicine. It will assist in the practice of doctors working in gynaecology, venerology, family planning and general practice, their nursing colleagues and in disciplines engaged in psychotherapeutic work and counselling. Those working in the Health Science professions, if not able to offer therapy themselves, may be alerted to the need for an appropriate referral for their patients and clients.

Part One

CASE PROFILES OF DEVELOPING SEXUALITY

1

Early problems

Vaginismus
Anxiety
Promiscuity

Some years ago Anne-Marie, an au pair from a small pro-
vincial town in France, found her way, timidly, into a family
planning clinic in a residential suburb of London and met
one of the first doctors practising what has come to be called
psychosexual medicine, when the discipline was in its
infancy. The nurse receptionist, a motherly, middle-aged
woman, told the doctor later that the patient had twice put
her head round the door and withdrawn. Finally she had
blurted out: 'My lady said the doctor here will help me but
I think I am wrong here: I am not for pills, I have no
boyfriend'. She was lucky with her welcome as many recep-
tionists in those days would have turned her away but she
came in, hesitantly, with encouragement.'
Anne-Marie was young, beautiful and apprehensive. She
struggled to find the right words. 'I am sorry for my English
— I am here as au pair — my lady says you will help me
but I know I can never make babies — I am not *normale*
(pointing), 'there, *vous comprenez*, inside.' Clearly with this
beginner's English and the doctor's kitchen French, no
subtlety of psychotherapy was possible. But the nature of
anxiety was to some extent already perceptible from her
manner. Here was no sophisticated young woman looking
for protection or for factual information. She presented with
a real terror of an imagined incurable ailment. She was also
uncertain about her entitlement to help.
Encouraged to elaborate, Anne-Marie described how she
had tried to use tampons and failed. She was not told how
to use them, only that they were for married women. She

liked to swim, however, and had assumed from her failure that she was just not getting it right. She had heard of the 'hymen' and that it must be broken. Some of her friends, nevertheless, could use tampons without difficulty.

She had come from a warm, loving Roman Catholic family, who were not too strict, and was the eldest of her sisters. When at sixteen she and the boy next door fell in love, both families were delighted. The engagement was announced a year later, before he left for college.

At this point the shyness returned and after a long pause and with some embarrassment, she said: 'We have tried, you know, loving, and we could not — not after several times, and he had to go away, and we thought it was because we were young, but when he came back, still nothing, and he could do it with another girl . . . and we broke up . . . .' Tears flowed freely now. 'And we were all sad, and the families sad, and they could not understand, for we love each other, and we could not tell them.' Anne-Marie, however, had courage and she told how, 'though I am not like that kind of girl', she had felt she might learn from a more experienced boy. In another town she met an older graduate, who was nice but attempts to have intercourse were not more successful. He had told her truly there was '*un bloc*'.

Non-consummation due to vaginismus No conventional medical history had been taken, but it was immediately evident from Anne-Marie's story — indeed in her very manner of presentation before she had spoken — that she had many of the characteristics which are classic symptoms of non-consummation due to vaginismus, or spasm of the muscles at the entrance to the vagina. It is a problem which prevents thousands of young, and not so young, women from making that confident step into womanhood which the achievement and enjoyment of penetration implies.

This brief ten minutes of clinical study of one healthy young woman and her pain involves addressing a fundamental issue, not only for therapy but for an overall view of human sexuality. Was Anne-Marie's problem to do with her reproductive system or was it a problem presented by an anxious person, expressed in involuntary tension of this particular part of her body?

Western society, at least for the last 150 years, influenced certainly by the more prohibitive aspects of Judaic, Islamic and Christian teaching, has seen sex largely as a physical function, to be regarded, if not negatively, as something to be kept under control. So, for Anne-Marie and for many people who grow up in loving but protective families with caring parents whose approval is needed, there is an inevitable feeling of caution, albeit unconscious, about the legitimacy of the wish to become adult sexual beings, enjoying sex as part of maturation. The awareness that these parts of the body are developing in adolescence, discovered sometimes through the private, tentative exploration of masturbation and through powerful and exciting emotional desires and longings, is a natural part of personal growth. The ability to let it blossom freely and confidently depends to a considerable degree upon the inner confidence that this is a good aspect of development; that parental values are not so opposed to it that the 'good loving daughter' or 'good loving son' part of us cannot still feel loved and approved should this pleasure be experienced in the growth towards adult independence.

Legitimacy of sexual wishes

Anne-Marie's background, which was in no way unusual or pathological, played its part in her uncertainty. It was no accident that it was especially difficult to consummate a relationship which was openly known to her family. Incidentally, this may not have helped her boyfriend either. He found it easier with another girl, unknown to his parents, who may have mattered to him less.

Nor was it an accident that Anne-Marie hoped that a secret lover might be better for her, and that one of her first tasks, away from her background, in a new country, was to seek help in this matter. A body of opinion holds that the general practitioner should be the sole adviser on contraception and sexual advice, but general practitioners are called 'family doctors' for good reason, because they are the doctors of the family. Young people with sexual uncertainties will not readily bring such problems to a place where they may sit in the queue beside their next-door neighbour, where the doctor is inextricably connected in their minds with the family ambience. It is easier for them to seek help from a stranger, who will be their personal confidante. The heated debate in the 1980s as to whether doctors should be compelled to tell parents of the daughter's visit was based on a failure to understand the emotional factors. A skilled doctor, far from reinforcing teenage rebellion, may so free the young patient of fears and confusion that he or she may be able to go home and share the dilemma with their parents.

As we move forward into the 1990s the problems of our times, particularly those of AIDS, and the greater recognition of the occurrence of sexual abuse, will lead to changes in social attitudes and pressures. However the experience of doctors working in psychosexual medicine is that the feelings individuals have built into themselves, usually based on childhood and family experiences, have the greatest effect on sexual happiness. Anne-Marie's difficulties might perhaps in today's climate have been presented as a fear of AIDS, yet the underlying problem, as we shall see, lay in her image of herself.

In his seminar's pilot study of a hundred cases with consummation difficulties such as Anne-Marie's, Michael Balint analysed the myth of the Sleeping Beauty, romantic as expressed by Tchaikovsky and the choreographers, but less so when encountered in the harsh reality of the consulting room. The Sleeping Beauty, like Anne-Marie, had loving and protective parents whom she also loved. They warned her of the dangers of penetrating objects, of being 'pricked'. When she did encounter the spindle, she fell into a deep sleep, and was surrounded by a defensive forest, until her parents were long dead. Even then, she did not awake and confidently set off in search of adulthood and a lover. She waited, sleeping, until Prince Charming could fight his way through the thicket, and awaken her with a kiss.

Had Anne-Marie felt more sure of her parents' blessing on her emerging sexuality she might have been even more persistent with her first lover; more certain that her failed attempts to explore her body and its desires were appropriate. She did keep trying. Some, with deeper reasons for self-doubt, dare not get so far. Yet if the sense of parental prohibition on overt sexual behaviour arises in adolescence in an otherwise secure young person, the harm is easily undone.

When Anne-Marie and the doctor had reached the stage of understanding together her uncertainty about her right to develop a sexual relationship, they could move on to explore her fantasy about her vagina. Anne-Marie was able to explain that she visualized the *bloc* as closed muscles, deep and impenetrable, through which nothing could get in or out, and that surgery to remove the hymen or even to stretch it would be impossible. She imagined quantities of tissue would need damagingly to be cut away.

The doctor, who had previous clinical experience of this, knew that Anne-Marie was also speaking, unconsciously, about the frightening and potentially damaging aspects of 'cutting away' or 'breaking through' her emotional defences. There is a precise body–mind language for those who are expecting their genitalia to be physically examined. At that unguarded moment — which is, in a sense, an anticipation of 'penetration', physically by a finger or speculum, emotionally by the revealing of a normally 'private' part — they may express, verbally or in body language, attitudes or phantasies about their genitalia which may accurately reflect their feelings about the inner, desiring, sexual woman in them also.

Thus, 'I think you may find I am too small' may not only mean 'I fear my body is too tight for tampons or may be hurt by intercourse'; it may also mean, 'I think the sexual woman in me is frighteningly small'.

This in itself may mean different things for different people. For one it may mean, 'I fear it is too young, too undeveloped a part of me. Unconsciously I am still an obedient daughter, not ready to own my sexuality and be an independent lover or wife.' For another it may mean, 'I fear unconsciously that my sexual defences may be damaged, torn down, by something that is going to be emotionally too big for me', accompanied by the idea that penetration, defloration, may be physically painful or frightening.

Further, this 'something too big' may not necessarily be the penis, or the fantasy rape-figure, or the vision of the man as 'big', meaning stronger, more powerful, in control. What some women unconsciously fear will be 'too big', if their defences are down, may in truth be the enormity or the insatiability of their own uncontrolled sexual desires which may be associated with guilt. Similarly, a woman who hints at undue fastidiousness — 'I am sorry I have not washed', or 'this must be horrid for you, doctor' — may be revealing her unconscious attitude not only to her genitalia and its possible infection, but also how she sees her desires: 'I regard my sexuality as meriting apology, or in need of cleaning before it can be shared or revealed.'

These findings, which can usefully be psychosomatically interpreted, have occurred so consistently at the anticipation of this examination that it is called 'the moment of truth'. It was once believed to be true only of women, but, in the practice of psychosexual medicine, it has been observed that men too may disclose a specific anxiety at an unguarded moment when undressing in preparation for this intimate examination of parts of the body which are normally concealed and which are usually called 'private'.

It is worth mentioning that this expression 'moment of truth' is sometimes used in relation to the bull-fighter's confrontation with himself. It is used therapeutically, not in order to teach the patient, male or female, how to engage in sexual activity with their partners, but rather to understand something of their inner attitudes to their own sexuality. If their attitudes can be freed, their sexual behaviour may be liberated also, not in terms of conforming to a norm of performance, but in terms of being able to see their sex as a means of personal expression. In a truly confident person, that expression will vary from time to time, partner to partner, mood to mood; indeed, in a truly confident couple, from moment to moment. Sexual expression, as distinct from sexual performance, is after all capable of showing many things: 'kicks', total spiritual communion, duty (not usually so good for either partner!), tenderness, friendship and comfort in trouble.

Having elicited Anne-Marie's phantasy, it was then a straightforward step to physical examination. Gentle examination of the trembling young woman revealed strong pelvic muscles, tight in terrified spasm. She was taught that they were under her voluntary control to tighten and relax at will and she was encouraged to feel inside herself and discover that once relaxed, once past them, there was plenty of room inside and the warmth and moistness was altogether agreeable.

She was amazed and delighted, and returned the following week having managed tampons without difficulty. She was, she said, *absolument assurée* that she would be able to make love the next time she wished. It had been the phantasy which had prevented her. And would she then like the pill, in case she met someone? 'Oh no, thank you so very much, I shall return for that only when I fall in love again. I think, for me, that is what it must be for, this excitement, no?'

This took 30 minutes. Not all women with such fears and such a background can respond so easily. For Anne-Marie, however, who had no partner, a programme of instruction in intercourse technique would have been useless. It is consistently found also that recommending self-examination and dilation of the vagina is futile if the phantasy underlying the fear or dislike has not been first elicited and understood.

Asking a girl who feels that her genitalia are unattractive to look in a mirror, for example, can only provoke a negative reaction. Assertions from the clinician that the patient's genitalia are normal and agreeable may only reinforce the helpless feeling that not only is she anatomically inadequate but that her anxieties are stupid too.

Ironically, the relatively new-found freedom to talk of sexual matters has resulted in a view of sexuality that is still dismally near to the 'purely physical' view of the puritanical past. The difference is that now it can be reduced to the merely physical and the 'healthy'.

Kinsey and his otherwise admirable questionnaires may *A sexual* have unwittingly suggested a 'norm' of sexual behaviour. *norm* Masters and Johnson with their otherwise admirable experiments may also have unwittingly set a 'norm' of physiological response.

For the uncertain, this may create a feeling that there is but one standard. Young people, who are normally anxious to be at one with their peers, are led to believe that sexual satisfaction comes immediately. The young are under increasing pressure to gain early experience. Those who do not find it so easy, which probably includes the majority, may believe themselves to be at fault, not realizing that there must be a learning, exploring time as with any worthwhile human experience. They must find what is right for them and acquire the confidence to become selective.

Inability to allow penetration, as experienced by Anne-Marie, is only one kind of difficulty in early sexual life. Other people, in their difficulties in finding love and expressing it sexually, can produce totally different symptoms from similar uncertainties arising from their view of themselves.

Linda reached her twentieth birthday during London's 'swinging sixties'. A poor achiever at her Northern grammar school, at odds with her respectable middle-class parents, she had come, like thousands of her generation all over the

western world, to 'find the action', to do her own thing in
the big city. Little has changed since then.

Sadly, as for so many, Linda, short of money and without
qualifications, found that the harsh world of bedsitter-land
and hostel-land was bleak and lonely and a far cry from the
dream. From the age of sixteen she had begun to hang
around for company, first the coffee-bars and rock venues,
then the pubs and the even seedier clubs. Later she thumbed
rides on long-distance lorries, where a brief 'feel up' in the
cab would, with luck, buy a coffee and a fry-up on the
motorway. Linda had been luckier than some. Some of her
'rides' wanted little more; some indeed were family men
who would pat her behind and buy her a coffee and bid her
'Why don't you just get on home lass?'

The pill was now well established in most clinics and
surgeries, as was the principle of contraceptive advice for
all who sought it. A few older clergy wives and Mothers'
Union representatives had handed over their valuable
pioneering work to a new generation of clinic workers. It
was one of these more trendy young women that Linda met.
Linda, however, was almost too much even for her. Her
jeans were dirty, the lank peroxide hair hung in curtains,
concealing her eyes and most of her spotty face. The leather
jacket was flecked with cigarette ash and she smelled of stale
sweat and stale marijuana.

Despite her usual tolerance, the receptionist showed Linda
in with barely concealed contempt and distaste; 'This girl says
she lives "on the road", and has had one baby already'. The
language barrier for this doctor was different from that of
Anne-Marie. Linda, though English, spoke through a wad of
gum and chain-smoked hand-rolled cigarettes. Her sullen,
mid-Atlantic, hippie-Cockney accent was not easy to follow.

She told how she had indeed had a baby, born prema-
turely at seven months. It had died. 'Well, I had an eclamptic
fit, didn't I?' The doctor was shaken. Even basic ante-natal
care should have prevented this. How could it have happened? Linda's busy parents ran a boarding-house, and
didn't notice the children very much. She was not aware
she was pregnant at first . . . 'Well, like, at sixteen you don't
know where to go, do you?' She was seven months pregnant when she collapsed with a fit. Nobody had noticed her
condition before this.

The doctor remarked that it must have been rotten
for her. She responded with a first hint of interest and

surprise and one brief straight look: 'Anyway, I don't want that again, do I?'

The baby, she admitted shyly, had been a girl. 'Actually, they weren't going to tell me or let me see her . . . said what was it to me? . . ' While examining her before prescribing 'the pill', the doctor asked if she had a steady boyfriend. 'No, I take what I can find.' Asking whether she had regular checks for infection, she noticed that her underwear was clean and neat as were her genitalia. 'Oh yes, I'm very particular about that sort of thing, I'm not a scrubber, you know,' she said offendedly.

The doctor asked 'And do you enjoy sex then?' Linda now sat up, threw back her hair and looked the doctor in the eye with genuine astonishment. 'Enjoy it — I never enjoyed it. But you've got to, haven't you, if you ever hope to keep them. And if you can't keep them, I mean, how can you have any chance one of them might love you one day?'

This was the first of three consultations over a two-month period in which doctor and patient discussed Linda's ideas about this thing that men and women do behind closed doors. In Linda's view, this was the route to love if you were lucky.

Her need to seek for an accepting love of this kind had *Not* evident roots. Despite the protective respectability of her *enough* home, there was little expression of parental love by physical *love to go* warmth or verbal encouragement. With a busy lodging- *round* house and several younger babies, there simply was not enough personal cosseting to go round. Linda, as the eldest, had had to manage for herself from an age when she was too young to understand. She had noticed her parents often kissed and cuddled each other, but in the absence of any formal or loving sex education she had felt 'they kept it for themselves . . . it was for baby-making — and if I wanted it I'd have to grab what came'.

Hence the premature, in more senses than one, preg-nancy. Hence the inability, once pregnant, to 'bother them' with a cry for help. And hence the feeling that her vagina and its desires were very little to do with her, just a necessary evil in a total lack of pride in her own self-image. However, she 'kept it nice' and hoped it would one day, magically, bring her love.

Linda, and many girls like her, who embark on a life of disastrous promiscuity, have never reached orgasm and have rarely achieved any pleasure beyond the reassurance of feeling 'wanted'. Those few who do find their need for closeness sometimes carrying them to physical satisfaction often complain of feeling disgusted with themselves after a casual encounter. Such girls, who today do indeed run a serious risk of contracting AIDS and other sexually transmitted diseases, are not likely to be changed by campaigns designed to deter them from having sex. Their need for love is too great, and their sense of self-worth too small.

The true tragedy of Linda's story is that far from finding love or giving or receiving pleasure, such girls, and indeed many boys in similar conditions, find their sense of their own worthlessness simply reinforced by each unsatisfactory encounter. Each subsequent attempt to try again, to do better next time, is increasingly doomed. They take their inner problems with them, multiplied.

A doctor to help her enjoy sex   With Linda, the doctor took a positive line: 'What a waste! you have a lovely body, you keep yourself clean and fresh and, deep down, you have high hopes. Surely you can do better than that? If you are going to make love, let me help you to do it well.

Linda found it hard at first to believe that this middle-aged woman would want to help her enjoy sex. To begin with, her sideways stare made the doctor begin to feel quite disgraceful to have suggested it. She had to draw upon her psychotherapeutic knowledge to make some useful interpretation about the role of the 'mother'.

It was with delight and surprise that, three months after the third consultation, at which they had parted with a warm handshake, and 'Thanks a lot — I guess it's up to me now, isn't it?', the same receptionist said, 'Linda is here to say hello. She's brought you a present. She's just passing through', and then quietly, 'You won't believe it . . . It's *that* Linda. I didn't recognize her'.

Linda came in, a little embarrassed, still tentative about her entitlement to claim attention. She didn't want to be a bother. 'I know how busy you are.' But what a Linda! Her hair was shining, her skin was clear and the mascara, in the style of the day, was a little heavy. Her trim mini-skirt offset her long legs in high pink boots. In her evident happiness, she had a kind of beauty. An engagement ring, shyly edged onto the desk, was not mentioned.

Linda related that, with someone 'who had been just a pal' in the flat below for some time, she had 'loved it', and she had 'come' on several occasions and that it was worth waiting for. He had found her a job in his coffee bar and she was proud of the fact that he would not let her out from behind the counter. He was not going to allow all the other chaps to chat her up as they were going to be married. She had told him about the baby and his response was 'What a shame! We shall have to make another one, maybe a boy this time'.

Her present for the doctor was a tiny, dainty glass vase that might hold one rose. The symbolism of the gift was very apt. Gary was waiting outside and took Linda's hand. They did not look back.

2

Fantasies, phantasies and misconceptions

Maturation
Phantasy of smallness
Masturbation
The need to value phantasies

Mature 'Adolescence' is defined by Chambers as 'passing from
sexuality childhood to maturity'. From the study of many women
such as Anne-Marie and Linda, one may take a view of
adolescence in those terms which is unrelated to age or
physical development, but rather to the person's emotional
view of themselves. I have met women with similar problems at the age of thirty, forty, fifty, and older. Later, as
gradually men began to come forward for sexual help, we
met many of them too, of all ages, who were having difficulty in taking that emotional step. To pass sexually from
childhood to maturity requires sufficient internal freedom
from parental values, be they actual or perceived, and
sufficient freedom from the wish to please or to rebel against
such values, as to feel sure that one's instincts and desires
are one's own. Any unconscious difficulty with this maturation process can lead to sexual problems, as well as to other
emotional or psychosomatic problems. Without such freedom, both men and women can be sexually 'children' to
a greater or lesser degree all their lives.

These observations lead us also to a view of sexual difficulty and its treatment which must distinguish between
human sexuality and human sexual behaviour or performance. If individuals can be freed to own, without disturbance, their desires and instincts, in a way that feels right
for them, they will be able to use their instincts to 'perform'
and 'behave' sexually as they wish, with whom they wish.
If they lack a partner, they may be freed to make an appropriate choice of one, or to elect not to; they will be spared,

however, the dilemma of Anne-Marie, who felt herself so abnormal as to find difficulty in daring to try again. Or they may be spared the difficulty of Linda, who regarded herself as so worthless that she felt lucky to get anyone, and that any partner would do. Both these young women were in trouble with their adolescence, yet their sexual symptoms — virginal anxiety for Anne-Marie, loveless promiscuity for Linda — are at face value, in terms of their sexual behaviour, poles apart:

The other common factor for these two girls is that each had a specific view — a 'phantasy' — about the emotional nature of their sexual difficulty which was expressed in terms of a view of their sexual anatomy. The phantasies which both women and men have of themselves are of infinite variety, but many are so directly descriptive of the physical nature of the genitalia or of intercourse that the view they convey of their inner femininity or masculinity needs little interpretation in treatment. However, we have found that without eliciting the precise nature of the individual source of anxiety and respecting it, confrontation by insisting upon a different view of reality — our view — proves meaningless to the patient.

Most dictionaries give the words 'fantasy' and 'phantasy' identical meanings. Here I use 'fantasy' to mean 'daydream'; the conscious if unrealistic idea of a Walter Mitty or an adolescent in masturbation; a vision or scenario which can be conjured at will. It may be exciting to imagine, for example, being chased through the woods by some unattainable person of our dreams, or in giving chase ourselves. If chase it be, what happens at the end of it may also be the subject of fantasy. Not every day-dreamer would wish actually to be caught, and the vision of how it should end will depend to some extent upon practical knowledge of sexual matters, for the rest upon personal preference. If the fantasy of an uninformed youngster is too far from the practical realities, confrontation with those realities may come as a rude shock. There is a dilemma here, for masturbation can be a healthy and useful learning phase. How else may people begin to perceive and enjoy what their sexual organs and their desires are about? By full intercourse at younger and younger ages? Hardly, for emotional maturity too is required if early experiences are to be rewarding. But if a specific masturbatory fantasy becomes too crucial to enjoyment, and is too far from the reality of adult sexuality,

individuals may find themselves in trouble with a real partner in the real act. Furthermore, masturbation in some ways
offers the best of all possible worlds, since we may fantasize
whatever we wish and come to know exactly how to attain
climax with it, with no-one to interfere. When a partner
becomes involved he or she will be extremely lucky if they
chance to hit upon just that, whether in bodily or mood
terms. So masturbatory fantasies can be useful if we are
sufficiently confident and guilt-free to use them to convey
our preferences. Sadly, this natural development is often
so shrouded with shame that it is difficult to admit to. But
in therapy we can ask a patient, 'What are your fantasies?'
and they can answer if they wish.

In contrast I use the spelling 'phantasy', for purposes of
distinction, to mean something less conscious and possibly
pathological or distorted. In psychosexual medicine, when
we speak of 'phantasies being revealed' at, for example, the
moment of genital examination or in response to a verbal
interpretation, we do not just mean asking a pertinent question of someone whose guard is down. Rather we perceive
an idea, an image perhaps, about the body and its desires
which the patient may convey verbally or in body language
without being fully aware of it, but which may nevertheless
give clues to the nature of the difficulty. We learn to listen
for communications of this kind which could never be
dredged up in response to a straight question requiring a
factual answer.

As usual, case examples may illustrate the difference.
Arthur, of whom we shall hear more in the next chapter,
believed his penis was small though it was not: a conviction which represented his phantasy of himself as a 'small'
person in other ways. When this was interpreted to him he
no longer felt this misapprehension.

Alice:
phantasy
of
smallness
Alice, a biology teacher who could have turned to any of
her text books for the facts, revealed at genital examination
the phantasy that she was too small for intercourse by flinching in fear. She felt she had only one small opening
through which all dirty things came, though rationally she
knew this was nonsense. It emerged that she had had
repeated painful and frightening catheterizations for cystitis
in childhood, so that it was not surprising that the idea of
penetration by something as large as an erect penis should

recall her earlier bad memories. Only when she had been encouraged to express the childlike phantasy was she able to feel inside herself and be confronted by the reassuring fact that her vagina was amply elastic and her small separate urethral opening not at risk.

In contrast Kevin had fantasized since his guilt-ridden and lonely adolescent masturbation that the means to climax was to rub his penis around the umbilicus of his dream woman, with the penis in the downward (between the thighs) position. He and his dream would blend together, neither moving. He could reach orgasm like this snuggling into a soft mattress, thus also minimizing the risk of being overheard. When attempting to consummate his marriage with a girl who hoped for children he was in difficulty. So strong was his need for this particular fantasy that an eager moist vagina was unattractive by comparison and he would slip back to the abdomen at the moment of impending penetration. Though he rationally hoped to consummate and conceive, he had not been helped by treatment when I last heard, and his wife was finding it hard not to resent the 'wasteful mess', as she described it. *Kevin: masturbation fantasy too strong*

Khalida, a young Muslim bride born and bred in England, sensibly went to her GP when consummation was difficult. She rejected vaginal examination only because she felt her husband should have the right to 'first entry', so she was referred to a gynaecologist who stretched her under anaesthetic and assured her that all would now be well. She may have been normal physically but emotionally she could still not allow penetration. Her upbringing had led her to believe there must be pain and bleeding at first penetration, or she could not be a virgin. Earlier self-exploration, when her school-fellows began to use tampons, had allowed her to slip a tentative finger in with no difficulty. She was confused by this, did not dare to ask, and thereafter consciously decided that she had somehow 'spoiled' herself by some unremembered masturbatory activity. Shown by the doctor that her hymen was still present but elastic, and that bursting through with bleeding was rarely necessary even though some might find the idea exciting, was a great relief. Her young husband was encouraged to explore and stretch *Khalida: husband's right to first entry* her under the doctor's guidance. The knowledge that she was still a virgin helped them both considerably more than the 'reassurance' that she was large enough. Her husband, also Western-educated, had felt very threatened since both families held him responsible for the failure, and his erections had begun to flag in the face of his wife's spasm and his own reluctance to cause her pain. They had no further difficulty once the facts were understood.

Phan- A phantasy so widespread as to qualify almost as folklore
tasies is that a vagina can be 'too small' for a penis. While a
must be rigid hymen or the spasm of vaginismus can make the
valued entrance tight, a small vagina as a cause of intercourse difficulties is virtually always inaccurate. If we take it at face value, we may observe that the vagina is sufficiently elastic to allow the passage of a baby's head. I have yet to see an erect penis comparable in size, and if one exists it will certainly not have bones in it. So-called 'disproportion' in labour relates only to the bones of the pelvis, in relation to the baby's head. Episiotomy is performed only to avoid tearing of the perineum. How has such a common misconception come about? Doctors must take some responsibility. It is almost beyond belief — since they at least must be aware of the facts just stated — that they sometimes make such heedless comments at examination as 'You are rather small', or 'You may have difficulty in intercourse — or childbirth'.

Many anxious patients hear what they fear to hear, and we need to accept such stories with some reservations. However, Dr Jules Black, an Australian gynaecologist interested in sexual problems, found that doctors were reported as one source of this idea in a staggering 59% of his vaginismus patients. Furthermore, it is still by no means unusual for women to be given anaesthetics for stretching or removal of the hymen, or even full ('Fenton's') muscular resuture without the psychosomatic causes of the spasm having been explored first. Such patients' inner phantasies remain, of course, unless treated. They need to be elicited and faced consciously before they can be 'buried', in Tom Main's words, 'with full military honours'. He adds: 'Sexual phantasies are not usually matters of pride for casual public discussion, and the individual may well be aware that though precious and highly personal and meaningful for

him or her, they are also absurd and illogical; even ridiculous
in the light of common sense. To deride a patient's phantasies or dismiss them as absurd can only add to the scorn
the patient may already feel towards these private wishes.
Before they can contrast them with reality and then discard
them, he or she must be allowed to value them; to have
them respected and to be sad at parting with them as old
friends, or at least as secret parts of ourselves.'

Partners of women with vaginismus are not helped if their
own fears of causing pain are reinforced by the idea that
there is cause for surgery, or that penetration requires full
general anaesthesia.

Cathy was a young woman with an extremely rare condi- *Cathy*
tion: congenital absence of the uterus. Her vagina was only *and*
about 1½ inches deep and the entrance only just admitted, *Caroline:*
in virginity, one finger-tip. Tragically, of course, she would *need for*
never have babies, but she learned to stretch her hymen and *physical*
control her muscles like anyone else, and intercourse was *treatment*
enjoyable and orgasmic. Her vagina was small, but as always
elastic. Caroline, an aristocrat, was by contrast 76 years old
when her husband — let us call him the Colonel — was 84.
In a doctor's waiting-room he came across a book about sex
in the over-sixties and came home, as his lady reported with
amusement, 'full of the joys of spring'. Since her menopause
their marriage had drifted away from active sexuality into
a companionable sharing of the joys of their garden and their
many grandchildren. Deprived of oestrogen and exercise,
her vaginal entrance had indeed lost its elasticity and
contracted to about the size of Cathy's. Attempted intercourse was painful and led to soreness and bleeding.
However, with oestrogen cream and the same exercises that
helped both Cathy and Anne-Marie, all was well. Giggling
a little, like a shy but flirtatious debutante, Caroline reported:
'He's such a dear old sport, d'you know . . . One wants
to be matey!'

Women's phantasies are infinitely variable, but ideas of *Infinite*
potential hurt and damage are widespread. For some there *body*
is a frightened excitement about this, as though it ought to *phan-*
be painful, at least the first time. If this phantasy is not *tasies*
recognized, defloration by surgery or dilators is almost,

though not consciously, a disappointment. The muscle spasm returns, awaiting in certain, fearful, excited anticipation the 'real thing'.

Others fear that all manner of things — tampons, diaphragms, dilators, penises — will go into some 'wrong place', or be unable to get out. Again the confrontation of phantasy with fact by self-examination can be therapeutic only if the specific fear has first been verbalized and understood. Others still find difficulties in ideas of dirtiness, messiness or impropriety. Instilled in the 'dirtiness' of touching, they have found it hard to dissociate the vagina from the excretory functions of 'down there'. One referred to the proximity of the vagina to the rectum as 'like a temple built over a sewer'; a graphic simile, but hardly conducive to a sense of beauty or romance. Still others have less than rational phantasies that the entering thing, the penis itself, may be harmed or trapped or 'dirtied' by their own view of the place it is to enter. These ideas too have their parallel in the concept they imply of a woman's inner sense of her sexual desires as dirty or dangerous.

Many men too see penetration as potentially damaging or frightening to their beloved, frail (as they see it), vulnerable girl. This does not help them maintain the necessary confident, steady but non-forceful erection or, in emotional parallel, firm patience, which is even more necessary than usual with a partner in frightened vaginismus. In their protective panic, they either struggle or stop. Staying steady is more likely to work. Here Masters and Johnson's [4] non-demanding persistence can be extremely useful, helping to dispel the mutual fear of further failure by removing the performance-orientated 'goal' of 'penetration or nothing'. But if the phantasy fears are understood, such a lengthy regimen is rarely necessary.

Other men fear being 'damaged' or stuck themselves, or going into the womb or the rectum or a vast welter of nameless abdominal contents the size of a full-term baby's uterus. The common phantasy that the vagina itself is threatening; that it even has 'jaws' or teeth that will close on the penis like a clam, has almost become a joke. It is true, however. Some men do have such barely conscious phantasies, and it is no joke to them. Again, the body–mind parallels may often be usefully interpreted and understood. A man may be helped to see that his terrifying vision is not only of the mechanical facts of intercourse, but also of what it represents to him in terms of his own desires in relation to what he sees as powerful, grasping, insatiable women. If he can be helped to see why particularly he has nurtured the phantasy (women are, after all, all-powerful to all men at some stage of their development, if only in the granting or witholding of the breast), the confrontation with the reality of his woman's body may be equally effective. Other men have anxieties about the 'dirtiness' of the vagina, and of their own feelings about it, and yet others see their own penis or emission as dirty or soiling to the partner.

Perhaps this is the moment to mention that in phantasies about the penis, size is almost always inaccurate. Men, like women, may have their own dissatisfactions about their appearance, but from the point of view of satisfying a woman in intercourse we only have to review the nature of the vagina to see that size is relative to requirement. Since the vagina is a closed elastic space, contact and thus stimulus is only achieved when whatever is inside it stretches it just enough, be that a finger-tip going in or a ten-pound baby going out. Yet men — and their partners — often truly believe that their penis is too small for a certain woman. This can lead too to the converse notion that a woman is too big, particularly after childbirth. It is true of course that close to orgasm there is dilation and 'gaping' in the upper reaches of the vagina. But this comes at the point of no return. Were the penis 'too small' that degree of arousal would be unlikely to be reached.

The size of the penis

Penis size, like vaginal size, varies somewhat but not much. Less confident men do seem to notice, more than most people, those illustrations which suggest that a normal erection is of enormous proportions, and at an acute angle to the abdomen. It would be preferable if more emphasis were placed on the variation; on the fact that a perfectly adequate erection may be at right-angles, or even below that, to the abdominal wall, especially in the older man. Many anxious men, or their partners, who have come to feel for their own inner reasons like slack 'old bags', seem prone to notice representations of anatomically improbable 'ideals'.

Generally speaking, a penis is as big as its erection and an erection is as big as its confidence. The adaptation of any penis, however 'small', to any vagina, however 'big', occurs automatically in every willing and confident attempt at penetration. If not, it is more likely to require exploration of the *sense* of feeling big or small than their anatomical measurement.

To be helped to take a cool clear conscious look at such ideas and thus to develop insight is the first step in this psychosomatic approach. Only if an individual cannot respond to interpretation of such phantasies will it be necessary to examine why he or she has been unable to make such discoveries for themselves. Often a sense of needing parental encouragement is obvious from the way the patient evokes such a response from the doctor. If I find myself treating an adult like a frightened child, or like an innocent who cannot be expected to find out the facts of life for themselves, I wonder with them why they require positive encouragement from outside themselves.

That many do is richly exemplified in rituals and marriage customs. The Jewish ceremony entails the symbolic breaking of the glass; the Anglican church asks the bride to step forward from her father's side to that of her husband-to-be. It is ncessary as we step forward into mature sexuality to feel free enough metaphorically to say to our parents, and most of all to the parent voice in ourselves, 'Thank you for my upbringing. I love you. But now goodbye. I shall make my own life and return to you only when I choose, as an equal.' If we cannot do this, we may well choose partners who to some extent represent the unconscious hope for a substitute. It was no accident that Anne-Marie was not going to take pills just to prove something to the doctor; she was freed not to have to prove anything any longer to herself. Nor was it a journalistic trick to end Linda's story with 'They didn't look back.' They didn't in any sense. The doctor had had her appreciation and thanks — and her goodbye. Linda's internalized 'parents' were needed no longer.

3

Images of oneself
and others

Ejaculatory problems
Poor self-image
Sexual problems with the loved partner

The understanding of human nature is not helped, I believe, *Difficul-*
by the idea that all people of any group think or behave *ties in*
alike. In the bad old days when some official forms had a *seeking*
box for 'race', a friend of mine always took pleasure in *help*
writing 'human'.

The analytical psychologist Carl Jung developed the
concepts 'animus' and 'anima' for the male and female
aspects which exist in the opposite sex for all of us. How
far these conflict or push the individual towards homo- or
heterosexual orientation and preference, and how comfortable we can be with these parts of ourselves, is complex and
relevant in treatment. But the assumption that men — or
women — feel this or that simply because they are men or
women, can lead to misunderstandings in relationships. Of
course men and women are different, not only physically
but in the attitudes to their bodies and desires related to their
physical roles. These we can celebrate with *Vive les differences*.
But the danger of labelling a characteristic we dislike in
ourselves as 'male' or 'female', and then attacking it in
others, is as counter-productive politically as it is in bed,
and leads to ignorant chauvinism.

We have found that the difficulty in finding the courage
to seek help is often directly related to the nature of the
individual's problem. Thus a woman whose difficulty with
orgasm is related to her doubt that to have positive active
sexual desires is legitimate will not find it easy to show a
desire for help either. A woman who finds it difficult to
abandon herself totally in uninhibited trust to her partner

in bed, will for similar reasons find it difficult to come openly and dependently to a therapist saying 'Please help me'. And it is true in general in our society that a woman can admit to a neighbour or friend that she does not enjoy sex without too much shame or apology; indeed to admit that she does enjoy it is sometimes more difficult.

In this work I am constantly hearing about girls who could or could not talk to their mothers about sex. Some wish they could, or could have. Others, who have picked up the common idea that if you can talk to your mother about it, it must be alright, are puzzled that they don't enjoy it despite the fact that 'I can tell my mother everything'. Yet why should it be necessary? However good the relationship, I usually find the thing the girl can say easily to mother is that she is having difficulty. Whatever the mother's own view, however understanding and encouraging she may be, it is quite unusual for a girl to go home and tell her 'I think sex is fantastic!' — especially if the unspoken communication behind that would seem to be, 'You were wrong, weren't you!' It is common to castigate parents for being too inhibited about sex; or, in the backlash, not conventional enough, so that the young are given no 'moral' values to kick against. It is my experience that whatever the parents say or do, the individual child will hear it or be deaf to it, obey or rebel against it, according to their individual capacity to do so.

Similarly, the difficulty that many men have in coming for help can itself be a reflection of the nature of their difficulty. Whereas individual men may be more or less pressured by it, it is true that in general men are expected, by women, by society, and most of all by themselves, to be confident lions in bed. It does not sound impressive for a man to boast at the bar of his club or on the football terraces, 'I was never much good at it.' Indeed not only are these images actually (and unfairly perhaps) part of the real pressures of society on a less than confident man, but they are also reflected in the facts of male sexual difficulty. An unresponsive woman can, if she will, 'lie back and think of England' or of the shopping list, and intercourse, however unrewarding for both partners, can occur. It is not so for a man in trouble. The practical athletics of intercourse are such that if a man's erection is inadequate, not only can nothing happen, but his difficulty is nakedly revealed and obvious in a way that his partner's need not be. This is one reason why many men find it more difficult and humiliating to admit their uncertainties, either privately or in help-seeking. Nor should we be surprised that those who are brought along for treatment by their dissatisfied partners should feel reluctant and defensive.

Alan was an approximate contemporary of Anne-Marie and Linda. He was 25 when I met him in the 1960s, in similar confusion about being a child of his time. He found his own way to me via his most recent girlfriend who had told him I was 'easy to talk to' over her contraceptive advice, and he said at once that their sexual relationship had been over for some time though they remained friends. He had not got around to getting to know anyone else lately. He was a bit scared that he would fail again and make a fool of himself. He only felt able to talk to this other girl because they had been mostly 'just friends'. Her steady boyfriend had been someone else. He'd felt comfortable confiding in her because 'she didn't expect too much sexually of him'. *Alan: premature ejaculation*

Alan, a graduate social worker, had shoulder-length curly hair in the style of the day, and a full beard to match, leaving not much of his face showing beyond the shy blue eyes, with a hint of tears not too far from the surface. He was dressed in jeans, sneakers and a flower-embroidered denim jacket, all spotlessly clean. I knew this 'uniform' went with a pacifist kind of idealism with its own folk music but he felt the need to explain at once, in an accent of the industrial North Midlands, that that was why he adopted this fashion. 'I don't think' he said, 'that it means I'm effeminate. But my father reckons so — a right Jessie, he says. He's a miner, you know.' His sexual complaint was that his first attempts, at university, were very nervous and had resulted in premature ejaculation, 'even in my trousers when she was trying to unzip me'. His embarrassment about this had increased at each subsequent attempt; and the problem, now that he feared and expected failure, had increased as well. His terror of these adventurous, to him apparently experienced, young women was manifest, and his humiliation at not being in command of himself had brought him to the stage when he hardly dared chat up anyone new. 'It looks as though my father was right, doesn't it! I'm sure I'm not homosexual, I love girls. But I do seem to be a bit of a wet . . . I wonder if I'll ever be a real man.'

We did not find ourselves talking much about his sexual performance after that first shyly blurted frightened outburst (not a bad metaphor for his sexual difficulty). I heard that he had been bright at school, inspiring great pride in his working-class parents.

Their evident (to me) joy in having a university son was tempered for him by the feeling that he had 'lost them' in the process of his education. His language had created a gulf; his academic achievement had left them behind. His admiration for his tough, less articulate, 'real man' of a father was shiningly clear — but the sadness that his father could not understand him, with his 'fancy ways', blinded him to his father's shy but uncomprehended pride. He went home less and less; missed them dreadfully; felt ill at ease, guilty, isolated, when he did. Yet he was modestly proud of his talents as a social worker and I could see he would be a good one. His sense of identification with awkward angry deprived youngsters, and their sense of alienation from loving authority, was rich indeed, though I felt sadly that he would have to learn one day how to combine this with the steady 'coal-miner father' image; that they too might need to learn to kick against someone who would love them just the same!

This was a funny kind of 'sex therapy' — no physical examination, just a couple of hours of talking together. My role was that of thinking on his behalf about things he could not see for himself, about what kind of man he was, and what kind he wanted to be. Perhaps I, as an academically successful person from his new world who could also enjoy and value the earthy inarticulate warmth of what he had left behind, was a useful model. He then went home for Christmas, and felt free enough to take a new girlfriend (a graduate colleague with, as he smilingly confessed, a 'posh' accent). They had 'got on fine'. He had checked the football pools with Dad, and they had taken the parents out for fish and chips on the Monday, so that Mum could stop trying so hard with her cooking. I never did ask whether his premature ejaculation had improved. It seemed irrelevant — indeed unimportant. If his demeanour in the consulting room was anything to go by, this young man was now in command of himself and enjoyed being so. It is likely that he would become that way in bed also.

Alan had in common with Anne-Marie (Chapter 1) a shy and tentative determination to find his own sexuality among peers who seemed to expect them to rush into confident sex without a moment's uncertainty. Both dealt with their problem not by frantic experimentation and boastful bluster, but by quietly working out why they could not fulfil their own ideas of how it should be.

Another worry of Anne-Marie's was that in common with many people of both sexes, her image of her body was that something about it was faulty.

Arthur was one of countless men who feel there is something not right about the genital itself. *Arthur: poor image of genital and self*

He was 28 when I met him and worked in the same High Street bank he had joined from school. He hoped, he said matter-of-factly, to make assistant branch manager one day, but did not seriously expect to rise higher. 'I think they are quite pleased with me. They know me as a responsible chap. But obviously' — laughing wryly — 'I'll never be a gnome of Zurich!' It was at this point that work began, on the poor self-image behind that 'obviously'. So often a whole life story can be seen not so much from a single word or phrase but from the attitude with which it is offered. Outwardly Arthur was a tall, slim, neat, articulate, eminently presentable young man. Certainly he blushed, sweated a little. It is not easy to come to a woman specialist and speak of intimate failures. Yet had I sought to put him at his ease by calling him Arthur and inviting him to call me Prue, as is common among some therapists, I would simply have reinforced the inequality of the relationship at that stage. Such an artificial attempt at 'equality' would have made me seem even more 'up there' and matronizing, he further infantilized.

From his one word 'obviously', then, expressed with total acceptance, we can observe Arthur's absolute conviction that he would never reach great heights in work or in life. The saddest thing of all for such anxious people is the way in which their low valuation of themselves affects their relationship with others — lovers, parents or employers — who might well be prepared to take a quite different view. They are so sure that they are worthless that anyone who finds them otherwise seems automatically suspect. Groucho Marx was speaking for countless men and women when he cracked 'I wouldn't want to belong to a club that would have me as a member'.

With this observed and interpreted, Arthur began to see that this poor self-image was to do with his childhood vision of himself. A brother who had been killed tragically in a road accident at the age of four — before Arthur's birth — had haunted his childhood like a much loved — better loved perhaps — ghost. Although his upbringing as an only child had been warm and happy, it was not surprising that his parents would be somewhat over-protective after such a tragedy, thus sowing the seeds of marginal doubts about his own capacity for independent strength and survival. In his teens he was thin and grew fast and began to learn about his emerging manhood through masturbation. His mother, naturally enough, fussed about his thinness, wrapping him up after football games and giving him vitamins.

At school a quite different dilemma confused Arthur's struggle for confident adult masculinity. Boys shorter than he pulled his leg and called him 'lofty' and asked, 'What's the weather like up there?' — all the usual teasing for an unusual member of a peer group. Some chaps, already more confident, might recognize the envy and feel free to notice not that they were odd to be tall, but that the others were unlucky to be short! Not Arthur. He looked down upon his penis from his great height, and upon theirs in the changing rooms on their smaller bodies, and saw his as 'small'. At the same time the inner bit of him which found masturbatory pleasure so good, so comforting, so exciting, felt guilty that it might be doing him harm. Something so secret and exciting must be both naughty and dangerous. We cannot call Arthur's (or his mother's) dilemma deeply pathological. Her experience had been that unprotected children do get into danger. Her reasonable terror and guilt about this, which got through to Arthur in years when he was too young to understand, were based on fact. His brother was dead, and in the circumstances her concern was quite understandable.

Arthur's symptoms were of premature ejaculation at his first shy attempts, resulting in a great sense of personal humiliation at his lack of control. This was aggravated by his sense of failing to please the girl. As with Alan and Anne-Marie, it was becoming increasingly difficult to dare to try again with the fear of further failure to dog his dreams for the future.

His sense of his own 'smallness' was pure phantasy, as I could see when, as often happens to men who are anxious and embarrassed in anticipation of showing their genitals to a woman doctor, his penis became powerfully erect. The phantasy had its emotional parallel in the feeling as a boy, despite his physical height, of being 'small' in the sense of needing extra care and protection and in his parents' very natural difficulty in allowing him to grow up. And finally, since he loved his mother and wished to please, he was in some difficulty with the rebellious independence-seeking part of himself which would have wished to respond to her over-protectiveness: 'Please just shut up and let me be my own man.' No-one who loves their parents would wish to say this overtly in words. We do, however, need to be able to say it to ourselves, to acknowledge the wish for rebellion and our entitlement to it, inside our own heads, without too much sense of guilt. Thus, before reassuring Arthur that his penis was normal in size and his erection as strong as any I had seen, it was necessary to help him see, in common-sense terms, why his lack of confidence in trusting his own instincts had roots in his actual life experience as he saw it, and implied no deep-seated psychological disturbance. We were examining together why it was that he had that 'small' vision of a perfectly adequate part, and of himself as a man.

Leroy: sexual problems only with the beloved

Leroy, like Linda and many other boys and girls, dealt with his adolescent doubts differently: by keeping trying in a way that even he felt was leading him close to a futile promiscuity, which resolved nothing in terms of his dreams, which were to 'make it' with a girl he also loved. Yet when he did fall in love with a girl he hoped to marry, all the 'stud' talents, which had served him well with girls who mattered to him little, deserted him, and he would ejaculate too quickly. Later, in his anxiety not to do that and fail her and himself, he began to lose his erection at the moment of attempted penetration. And this, he complained almost tearfully, happened only with his fiancée. He had never had a flicker of trouble with other, more casual relationships. How tempting then, as so many do who are in trouble sexually with their husbands, wives, or true loves, to assume 'incompatibility' and give way to despair. One of the hazards of this, as I believe almost always false, assumption is that to try elsewhere, whether with lovers or the surrogate partners provided by some therapists, usually *is* easier.

While the increased confidence so temporarily engendered may help at home for a time, it rarely does permanent good, in my experience, unless the reason for the difficulty — that the loved partner matters to them so much that they become over-anxious to please — is first understood. Prostitutes know this. They understand not only men's needs to feel good even when not performing too skilfully and when needing a bit of help, but the fact that 'love' can actually be a pressure.

Much misapprehension about the need for sexual variations exists in this area. As we shall see, oral sex, bondage, sado-masochism may all have their part in the sexual needs of individuals, and the intensity of those needs varies. At one extreme they may be a natural and acceptable part of fun and play for a couple who both enjoy them. At the other there may be real discrepancies of need, such as the kissing of the penis for a man whose partner finds this difficult. Or if the need for sado-masochistic practices is too great or too violent, it can be physically dangerous. Misunderstanding of the nature of such needs is not helped, I believe, by sex manuals which encourage the 'whatever turns you on' view to these lengths. They imply that 'straight sex' is dull; that truly sophisticated star lovers will dare more. The truth is that the more unusual needs often occur in those who have difficulty in enjoying conventional ways, and who need extra help to do so.

Leroy was 25 — handsome, hefty and black. He was a fine competitive athlete, a boxer in his spare time, and a keen disco dancer. His accent was Yorkshire; he had lived in Britain since the age of five as the eldest son of a family of nine children. His father, a casual labourer, had travelled much and Leroy had little memory of him until they had made their home here and Leroy had started school. He was a highly articulate and intelligent young man but, although he had a good white-collar job, his educational achievements were modest. Like all of us, he had intuitively found his own safe ground — in his case physical prowess — and had concentrated upon it. It was not surprising that he had plenty of choice among the girls at the discos and felt easy and confident with them. Nor was it surprising that among his athletic talents it was boxing at which he excelled. His view of it, however, was interesting. He did not see it, as I did, as a skill in violent contact: his special pride was in controlling and disciplining his bodily aggression. We were able to discuss the parallel between this and his confident sex as something of which he was in control. Conversely, uncontrolled outbursts, of which ejaculation is of course an example, made him uneasy when the wish to please made him feel that he was not in command. We could speculate together that the special anxiety about wishing to please a woman who mattered to him, and the added anxiety that her other boyfriends might have been better, could have roots in his childhood. He had, after all, been the 'man of the house' as the eldest son with an often absent father, until he was five — an age when we cannot conceptualize much, only feel and experience and be. The contrast — moving across the world to an alien cold environment, packed off to school, and no longer being the 'man of the house' — may well have created natural uncertainties which set the scene for uncertainty about his ability to please or be in command with the first girl he really loved.

I do not know whether Leroy was helped by our consultation. He did return once, smartly dressed in contrast with the studied, perhaps challenging, informality of his first visit, when he had seemed a bit sullen and defensive. He said blithely that things were 'better' without amplification, and, with great civility, paid me off and left. He was certainly more in command with me. But was this a sign that he was so at home also or was he merely putting me in my place for fear of further emotional exploration? It is hard for doctors not to know the results of our care if our patients decline to tell us, or refuse to give us credit if credit is due. Yet to demand acknowledgement is to deny the essence of our contribution. The signs of 'successful treatment' are patients who own themselves and for whom, like the 'parent voice' in their head, we have become irrelevant.

Our studies have shown quite consistently that the dilemma about the control of aggression and of the opposite — the 'uncontrolled outburst' — often occur in men with ejaculatory difficulties. Premature ejaculation is a very common symptom of anxiety about loss of command and control, though not necessarily of specifically aggressive impulses. Many men, however, find it difficult to ejaculate at all; many more can ejaculate in dreams, in masturbation or even by mutual masturbation with their partner, but not within the vagina. We frequently come across this problem

Ejaculation, control and self image

in gynaecological or sub-fertility clinics, where women may undergo a full investigation for sub-fertility before disclosing that their husbands are unable to ejaculate in the vagina. Since such men can often maintain their erection in the struggle for climax for long periods, resulting in prolonged pleasure and often multiple orgasms for their wives, the simple question 'Is sex all right?' may not reveal the true cause.

The pressure on both partners to conceive, to perform by the ovulation chart, may pose difficulty for a man, making him feel less wanted for himself than for his semen and turning his wife into a seemingly demanding and dissatisfied woman. In that situation both will inevitably feel some disappointment and tension. Sometimes overt marital warfare may break out and ruin the relationship. This can happen when infertility is responded to by artificial insemination by donor without adequate counselling beforehand. But for many men who have difficulty with orgasm because of unconscious fears of their uncontrolled aggression, the reasons must be explored before they can hope to ejaculate at will. Often such men have been close to a mother whom they have seen as powerful and hard to please, or they have had to take some responsibility for her beyond their years. Often their father has been absent or ill or otherwise shadowy, so that the model of how a steady potent man can deal comfortably and safely with powerful women has been missing.

Men learn to deal with this in individual ways, but often non-ejaculators channel their energies into selfless idealism: church-going, public service and so on. While admirable in itself, this need to deny the part of them which would say to a woman, 'To hell with you and your demands', hinders them in dealing confidently with necessarily explosive feelings in bed. Others are often strong powerful men, excelling in the hurly-burly of physical competition with other men with whom they can safely let rip physically and competitively without fear of doing harm. But with women, to whom they feel protective, they may fear the consequences of uncontrolled aggression, and nothing can happen. It is interesting that a woman doctor who tries eagerly to help such men ejaculate inevitably falls into the trap of becoming in the patient's eyes just another demanding woman, towards whom he fears his own resentment also. More than once such a man, if he has been helped to understand something of himself in this way, can ejaculate only after the doctor and/or the wife has given up trying, rather as infertile couples often conceive the moment an adoption is arranged. It seems even more likely that this can happen if both doctor and patient are aware of his need to tell her to get lost, and can see that the doctor at least can accept this without being destroyed. Thus the terror of saying 'boo' even quietly to a demanding woman may recede, and the need to keep control of his impending outburst and let ejaculation occur in more ways than one may be relieved.

Why, I am asked, do such men go to women doctors, when we are in the minority? Perhaps some men would choose otherwise, but historically 90% of qualified members of the Institute of Psychosexual Medicine are women, though in any new training group today the proportion of male doctors is much higher. But it is surprising how often men in sexual difficulty do seem to come to us women even when they have a choice. I have noticed different explanations for different men. Some find it harder to 'confess' their failures to a masculine 'rival'. Some know, as it were, that we women have all the power, as their mothers did. And some, I am uncomfortably aware, come to put us in our place, to defeat us! Quite unconsciously, of course . . .

4

The limits of brief psychosexual therapy

Boyhood encounters
Undecided sexual orientation
Help that came too late
Defeating women passively
The need to placate women

More It cannnot be stressed too often that to achieve intercourse
serious in the mechanical sense is a far cry from the enjoyment of
body it. Orgasm does not necessarily follow; nor will orgasm alone
image automatically ensure a confident sense of personal delight
problems in one's own sexuality. But before leaving the matter of simple
consummation, of body image problems and the 'ownership'
of adult desires, it would be dishonest to make even those
sound easy. Various factors contribute to the difficulties, and
not only that of the skill of the therapist. The patient's motivation for inner change — as distinct from wishing their outside circumstances changed — is crucial. So too is the age, or
the level of development, at which things began to go wrong:
when emotions began to need to be controlled or repressed.

Anne-Marie (Chapter 1) and Arthur (Chapter 3) had fairly
simple (when consciously understood) worries about their
image of their own bodies. Both sought help for themselves,
daring to be aware that something in themselves might be
helped with understanding. Other problems of body image
may be much more serious, and require deeper forms of
treatment which are beyond the capability of any sex
therapist or specialist in psychosexual medicine. Any
shoulder to cry on may give comfort, but this is not to be
confused with effective treatment. Doctors in this field must
know their limitations; they must make accurate diagnosis
and referral when necessary, if their patients are to trust
them. The limits are self-evident for, say, surgery. No-one

would expect a family doctor to perform open heart surgery on the kitchen table. But it is harder to grasp this obvious fact when the illness is an emotional one.

If our nearest and dearest has tuberculosis or a broken leg, we can see the problem and be sensitive as to what help is required, but it is harder to understand that people in psychological trouble cannot simply 'pull themselves together' and recover. It is sad that nearly a century after Freud's discovery of the unconscious, many still hear the label 'psychological' or 'psychosomatic' as a criticism rather than as a factual diagnosis.

This block can be a double-edged sword, not helping the patient and placing an unncessarily heavy burden upon those around them. Muddled, pseudo-psychological ideas that it is 'mother's fault' or 'husband's fault' make us feel guilty, and we try to change the patient's inner world by changing our own behaviour towards them. This may be admirable — but futile unless we are also aware that the patient's inner world requires professional understanding. Be kind, of course, to your son with his broken leg or your wife with her tuberculosis; be patient with them in their misery and awkwardness. But do not, surely, regard that as an alternative to the plaster of Paris or the streptomycin. Sympathy is no substitute for expertise.

A classic illustration of an illness which is at least partly *Anorexia* related to problems with body image and the adolescent *nervosa* struggle for independence, but which requires more intensive treatment than psychosexual therapy, is anorexia nervosa, together with the associated condition of bulaemia, compulsive eating. These conditions are often encountered by medical gynaecologists and family doctors, since the presenting symptom may be missed periods or difficulty in establishing a sexual relationship. It provides a good example, of which drug dependence is another, of the dilemma for the caring parent who feels that if they can only get their relationship right with their developing adolescent, the condition will be cured and that to have to seek professional help is somehow an admission of personal failure. Yet the parents' very wish to help — their suggestion that help is needed — may itself be heard as criticism by troubled adolescents. Ultimately, they must find their own motivation for help-seeking.

The breast as a focus for anxiety

Today cosmetic surgery is becoming increasingly — some would say dangerously — easy to obtain, at least for those who can pay. The breast is another common focus for anxieties about body image.

Those who for one reason or another feel uneasy about their appearance are very vulnerable, at times of stress or strife, to the idea that some physical change will help. At times of bereavement, or rejection, a woman in despair may, if her breasts (or indeed her nose, her genital apparatus or any other aspect of her physical being) seem unattractive to her, seek to have them changed. But such change will not help unless the reason why this particular item has become the focus of her dissatisfaction with her self-image is understood. Indeed if, for example, large breasts are diminished at the price of scarred breasts, the despair may be reinforced and she may be harshly confronted, unsupported, with the realization that her despair is within, inaccessible to surgery.

Most doctors have a few private nightmares about how they might have done better by a particular patient. The worst of mine is about a creative, lively, intelligent woman who came to me regularly for routine checks, and whom I came to think of as a friend. Her breasts were on the small side and she elected to have augmentation surgery although there was no medical necessity for it. She was delighted with her new shape, which was aesthetically lovely. As always in the presence of prostheses, it was difficult to be sure whether one was feeling anything unusual in examination, because of the firmer texture. Should I have suggested regular mammography? Perhaps in hindsight, but it was new at the time, and there was still some debate as to whether unnecessary radiation had its own risks. I did not do so and careful regular examination showed no cause for alarm. Yet when, only six months after the last check, the patient herself discovered a tiny lump at the edge of the prosthesis which was clearly suspect, it was found that a carcinoma had been growing under and hidden by it for some time. Augmentation surgery can make breast cancer harder to detect.

There is in my experience a psychosomatic language of the breast just as there is of the vagina. A number of women have complained to me of personal dissatisfaction with breasts which, to me, appear perfectly normal. I find this is sometimes related to their view of both themselves and their maternal role. A girl who feels her breasts are too small may also reveal uncertainty about her capacity to become a good mother, perhaps through having a poor model of good mothering from her own childhood, or from having had such a 'star' for a mother that she feels inadequate by comparison. Less often I have met women who feel their breasts too big, and for whom this seems to represent a sense of being too old, too motherly, at the expense of their personal youthful sexuality. Adolescents with large breasts often feel shy of them with reason. Many quite small girls find their breasts develop fast and early: 'They blew up like balloons', said one; another, 'It's like carrying a sack of coal in front of me.' They are self-conscious as their breasts shake about at gym classes, and they are vulnerable to leg-pulling by their schoolfriends, whose envy is unperceived.

There are some women who can take pride in their breasts whatever the shape, while others wish to change them. We may ask why, before deciding whether to recommend surgery. With a responsible family doctor, a reputable surgeon and above all careful psychotherapeutic counselling beforehand, the treatment may well be justified and may even be provided by the National Health Service. I am not against cosmetic surgery *per se*, but I do invite more caution about proceeding without careful exploration of a healthy individual's negative view of a particular anatomical part.

Short of surgery, it is worth noting that breasts, apart from pregnancy and lactation, vary in size only with the amount of fat they contain. The idea that one can easily develop bigger breasts without getting bigger all over is wishful thinking. When breasts are stimulated by hormones, the effect is more active — and thus often more uncomfortable — breasts. This will be at best temporary, at worst unwise.

It is unfortunate that cultural and media pressures imply that one shape is 'better' than another, when beauty, even in the eye of the beholder, comes in many shapes and sizes. The older generation were conditioned to the desirability of full breasts. This ideal gave way to slim boyishness, in Western culture, in the 1970s. Yet even with such pressures most people can be content with the body they have, and if they cannot, deeper problems may be involved.

Another problem with deep roots is trans-sexualism, the certainty that one is and wishes to be the opposite sex to that of the body one has. This condition too should not be expected to respond to simple psychosexual treatment, although acceptance and the opportunity to air pain and confusion may be supportive. Can we call this a simple problem of body image? If so, it must be the ultimate. Or is it a true delusion?

Nor can we regard homosexuality as 'treatable' in this simple sense. The Gay Liberation Movement would resent the suggestion that it might require treatment at all, and I do not intend to enter that debate here. Those homosexuals (and trans-sexuals) I meet professionally usually come for practical help rather than for change.

Homo- However, as this section is about early sexual experience
sexual it is worth a word, I believe, about those young people of
feelings either sex who are afraid of, or are confused by, their homosexual feelings. We all have the capacity to love, in various ways and to various degrees, others of either sex. Society has begun to accept that people who prefer their own sex as sexual partners are not to be condemned, but rather understood. Of course there are all sorts of affectionate relationships between members of the same sex. No-one thinks anything of two women kissing each other in friendly greeting, and in Europe this is also quite usual for men. In recent years it has become perfectly acceptable among members of a football team, and it seems to be practically obligatory between world leaders.

Since the word literally means 'of the same sex', every relationship between father and son, sister and sister, could be described as 'homosexual'. But we usually use it to mean that the partners express it and love each other in an erotic sense. Research has not established why some people of either sex find themselves preferring to be like this (as they would feel), or being unable to do otherwise (as those who regard it as pathological would feel). We do know that we all have the capacity to be capable not only of loving members of our own sex in the usual ways that I have suggested, but also of being attracted to them. Only when that aspect is so strong or so deep in our unconscious is it likely to cause problems in relating confidently to members of the opposite sex.

Perhaps the most uncomfortable people in present-day society are not those who are committed and admittedly homosexual in their way of life. It is often far more difficult for 'mostly' heterosexual people, who may be married or wishing to be 'normal' about the opposite sex but who find the homosexual part of themselves too strong for comfort. Such feelings can interfere with their sexual confidence with the opposite sex, making them feel confused, frightened and ashamed. It is a much more common problem than those who feel isolated and abnormal about it would believe.

Whatever the true causes of confirmed homosexuality, it is a universal and normal phase of adolescent development to feel some attraction to others of one's own sex, whether it is felt by boys for their heroes or for smaller boys in protective identification, or girls for their teachers. It is common to blame the enforced monasticism of boarding school or prison for much homosexual seduction, although whether these are cause or effect is debatable. If we would abandon the 'label' when considering the adolescent development of an individual youngster in his or her pain and confusion, we could develop some interesting and challenging approaches to sexual development.

James was introduced to homosexual masturbation at his boarding school. He felt dreadful about it, and privately labelled himself 'homosexual'. When he emerged as a 'deb's delight' at 19, he was so terrified at the idea that his shameful secret would somehow be revealed that he failed at his first intercourse attempts and failed increasingly thereafter. His generation was not that of demure debutantes. His girl contemporaries, also hiding their own uncertainties, clung together behind a much more daunting and 'sophisticated' kind of veneer. This foreign breed terrified James. It was clear that James, nanny-reared and lonely, had felt as an 11-year-old that it would be cowardly to cry or ring home and say, 'Please, Mummy, I hate it here, take me away.' He had found in his masturbatory cuddles with other boys the only warmth that he could, a primitive human comfort albeit guilt-ridden. Perhaps sharing this with an authoritative older woman who was undismayed was sufficient. I have met James since on other matters, but have not heard him mention homosexuality again, apart from stating freely, 'I can't believe how it used to worry me.'

James: boyhood cuddles the only warmth

Jerry, in contrast, with a different social background, had also believed himself homosexual from about 15, and with perhaps stronger reasons. He was aware that it was something to do with feeling that nothing he did would please or satisfy his police-sergeant father, for with a congenitally somewhat damaged foot he was inept at the tough athletic things his father gloried in. (No doubt that his father had his own feelings of pain and guilt about his beloved only son's disability, but that is another story.) In the event — and, as Jerry believed himself, in a spirit of rebellion 'That'll show 'im' — Jerry discovered 'cottaging' (picking up men in public lavatories for oral sex). He said that he never got much out of it apart from a good physical sensation and this secret glee at being such a rebel. However he had fallen for a pretty girl and thought of marriage. Not confidently potent with her, and with the same sense of having a terrible secret as James, he had confessed his past to a friend who advised him to join a gay club. His friend had taken his own diagnosis at face value.

It is advice widely given. For those who have come to be fully certain of their orientation, it may be good advice. For Jerry, however, it had crystallized his despair and his self-image, increasing not only his guilty confusion but his opportunity for 'easy' sex, at which he was confident. His self-disgust remained. His feeling of being inadequate with 'decent' girls was positively reinforced. Only his father's horrified discovery (when he had to explain the breaking off of his engagement), and the dismay it caused his ideal-ized mother, brought him for treatment. He was referred for and positively wanted psychotherapy. I hoped he might do very well. Was he homosexual, or was he, comparably with Leroy, someone whose early relationships had simply tipped him towards his own private confident ground, and given him secondary difficulty with a girl who mattered too much to him? We do know that, unlike James, Jerry was well on the way to accepting his own label and basing his lifestyle upon it. Maybe that will in the end prove right for him. He will, after treatment, at least make his decision for homo- or hetero-sexuality consciously — not out of rebellion and guilt, not simply, as James might have done, out of fear and failure.

Even people who are aware that their inner attitudes need help may feel so ambivalent, so fearful of the unknown consequences of looking inside themselves, that when their therapist helps them come near some emotional danger area, the 'cure' may truly feel worse than the 'disease'. Recognizing and respecting these defensive anxieties requires not only skill but courage on the part of both doctor and patient. There can never be total certainty as to whether a patient can use our interventions, and we sometimes fail them. We need always to try to do better. But for some patients, it seems, had they encountered even a modicum of psychosomatic understanding at their first help-seeking, their lives might have been transformed.

Elsie is a good example. She was 54 when I met her and *Elsie:* beginning to suffer the hot flushes of the menopause and *help may* the missed periods which signalled the end of her fertility. *come too* Beautifully dressed, carefully perhaps a bit excessively, *late* made up, her rich mahogany hair clearly restored, she was tense, weepy and even frantic. It would be easy to have diagnosed a simple menopausal depression, to have responded impatiently with, 'It's your age dear — you'll have to live with it', or, worse, 'You'll have to pull yourself together.' These contemptuous remarks had been made, according to Elsie, elsewhere. Since she had not received the minimum one might expect even from a purely physically trained doctor — an assessment as to whether there was treatable hormonal turbulence — one was tempted to believe her, and to acknowledge her despairing, rageful response.

Elsie had had consummation difficulties due to vaginismus when first married as a virgin to a virgin husband a quarter of a century earlier. I use the phrase deliberately, since it felt like a matter of centuries to Elsie — and to me. Despite her doubts about the legitimacy of wishing for sexual fulfilment other than for child bearing — which was the view of her upbringing, and not uncommon for that generation — she had persistently sought medical help. She had finally persuaded a surgical gynaecologist to perform a hymenectomy. It was not a success; nor was a fuller vaginal repair followed by instructions to practise with dilators at home. Attempts at intercourse had persisted all these years, and although this loving couple had found mutual sexual pleasure in other ways, the opportunity for conceiving the children they both longed for had now gone. Even at fertility investigations the fact of the continued non-consummation had not been noticed by the investigators. Perhaps we should not blame them entirely, for by then Elsie had clearly given up hope of consummation, and may not have shouted it loudly enough.

In parallel with the mechanical view of the gynaecologists she had visited earlier, who had believed that if the vagina was made bigger all would be well, a fertility specialist whom Elsie saw when she was about 30 had attempted artificial insemination with her husband's healthy semen — again without success, even though no other cause for infertility had been found. In cases of vaginismus, as with inability to ejaculate in the man, artificial insemination often fails, although the couple may conceive later when intercourse is naturally achieved. There are many fascinating emotional implications surrounding the dilemma of artificial insemination, whether by husband or donor, which merit further study.

Meanwhile Elsie, who was now too old for a family and with sexual enthusiasm fading in the light of her menopausal despair and her husband's increasing stresses at work, heard about psychosexual medicine and decided to have one last try. With the benefit of knowing what had failed to help before, it was clear within minutes that here was someone much like Anne-Marie, 30 years on. Elsie had a certain feeling — a phantasy — that her vagina was too small for the erect penis, certainly for childbirth. It had been reinforced not only by the sexual clumsiness of two inexperienced young people, but by a battery of 'experts' who took it at face value and reacted to it instead of understanding it. Her 'proper' upbringing, which told her that sex is something to be controlled, that young people are at risk from it and have to be careful not to allow their feelings to carry them too far too soon, had confirmed to Elsie the sense that penetration is a dangerous matter.

That feeling was interpreted to her as she approached the couch for yet another dreaded examination of these worrying parts. When shown that the muscles were under her conscious control, she burst into tears of amazed relief. She got down and checked for herself how they closed and opened on her own finger and agreed that now she could master the muscular trick, it was an exercise she could practise without her finger there to check. She would, they laughingly agreed, practise the 'twitch' whenever she could — on the bus, or watching the telly. She went home delighted — and so was her husband, for intercourse was not only possible but enjoyable within the week. Alas, the happy ending, which might have been achieved had she met someone so trained earlier, was not to be for Elsie. Despite her husband's continuing devotion, he had once or twice discreetly had a little sex-for-comfort flutter with a business colleague. This colleague, understandably perhaps, but disastrously for Elsie and her husband, was none too pleased that the light-hearted, as he saw it, liaison was no longer required. She rang Elsie in her pain and told all. Although there was little enough to tell, it was a bitter pill. It took a long time for Elsie to come to terms with her rage and depression over the children she would never have, over the wasted attempts to get skilled help earlier, and over this final straw of feeling let down yet again, this time by the person most important to her.

Two other quite separate people, Eamonn and Edward, both of whom were about 50 when I met them, also felt they had had raw deals from their medical advisers. As with Elsie, it was necessary to acknowlege their resentment of this and the ensuing difficulty in trusting another doctor, before work could begin. Technically, however, there was an interesting difference between Elsie and other such women, and Eamonn and Edward and other such men, as regards that crucial element in psychosexual medicine: the clues that come from the immediate doctor–patient relationship. Each individual approaches us differently and an alert doctor will notice that this provokes reactions in him or her which are unique to the patient, at that moment. *Using the doctor– patient relation- ship*

Thus with Elsie, her not fully conscious rage and disappointment evoked sympathy in her doctor which could usefully be observed with her and discussed. The danger of simply sympathizing with that identification would be to lose sight of the rich part of Elsie which was still trying and which felt there might be something she could change within herself.

Eamonn and Edward were, however, men! Since both, like Elsie, had tried a number of therapists and felt they had had very little help from them, it was both interesting and therapeutically important for me to notice that neither of these men was able to march confidently into the consulting room and metaphorically demand my credentials as someone who might have more to offer them. If the reader should feel that common civility would make this entirely inappropriate, I agree. Yet when, as their consultations progressed, I was able to point out how excessively polite and humble they were in dealing with such a terrifying monster as a woman doctor, each of them was able to laugh and admit that they were a bit like that with women in general, seeing them as powerful and to be placated. And for each this led, in different ways, to a fresh look at their reasons for needing to behave like this, and to a feeling that they might be occasionally entitled to direct a little righteous indignation, a little rebellious rage, towards powerful women. This was helpful — for there is a word for the feeling that there is nothing one can do in difficult circumstances. It is often called 'impotence', especially in the context of 'impotent rage'. People need to feel not too uncomfortable, unconfident or guilt-ridden about a positive entitlement to anger when dealing with awkward people.

Eamonn: defeating women passively
Eamonn was the eldest son of a good Irish Catholic family — he said 'from the bog', meaning from the country backwoods, but only the Irish themselves are entitled to make that joke. He said it apologetically but also with pride in his roots. Since his dream was to marry a virgin in church, the treatment he had received in a 'sex therapy' clinic, which included blue movies, exhortations to wilder masturbatory fantasies and advice to find a partner at a massage parlour, had only reinforced his sense of shame and even shock at his own sexual dreams and inadequacies. He was outwardly a well-built man, with red curly hair, bright eyes and the tanned freckles of an outdoor worker. He was semi-skilled but highly paid. One might have expected some sense of pride in a fine body — but on the contrary, Eamonn saw his erect penis as 'bent'. Several specialists had examined it — although not erect — and pronounced his vision 'nonsense'. The psychosexually-trained doctor, with psychosomatic language in mind, could have been tempted to wonder whether he was expressing a fear of homosexuality. Fortunately no such crass guess was made before examination. As often happens, the combination of talking about such intimate matters and anxiety about the physical examination produced a good erection, and it was possible to make a clinical, unembarrassing acknowledgement of its normality. It was clear that from the perspective of Eamonn's height his penis, with the weight of its strong erection, did indeed appear to

bend. It became easier for him to be able to accept reassurance that this was normal when the basis of his anxiety was accepted and discussed. He reported back next time that intercourse with his girlfriend had been possible — but only just. He had not much enjoyed it but gave the impression that if it was necessary for marriage, he would continue to do his best.

It was very tempting to feel that a miracle had been performed. In fact I then began to recognize how any feelings of success had been set up from the start by Eamonn's inability directly to criticize his previous therapists. Because of his need to show himself in a good light before a strange woman, I had been seduced into thinking that I could do better. To some extent this was true, for the mechanical behavioural techniques earlier applied had not included Eamonn's feeling that good Catholic boys, who love to idealize and wish to please a fantasy image of virgin motherhood in all women, do not have confident and vulgar sexual fantasies without guilt. Further exploration in the course of our consultations failed to increase Eamonn's positive enthusiasm for intercourse. He just did not positively enjoy being inside the vagina, which represented a symbol of the insatiable demands of women whom he must always deferentially do his best to satisfy. But his obedience represented two sides of a coin; for the vagina and its demands were also, it seemed, representative of the prohibited, dirty, sinful aspects of sexuality which his early family and church values made it impossible for him to enjoy without self-disgust.

The same self-disgust prevented him from responding to behavioural encouragement. One would have hoped that a psychosexual doctor's awareness of this, which Eamonn did seem to understand and temporarily respond to, should have helped more. It seems, however, that in trying to help, the doctor herself became inevitably in his eyes yet another powerful woman, to be placatingly obeyed. What I failed to perceive, and thus perhaps failed to help Eamonn to perceive, was that he could not be expected to enjoy feeling this way, humble and obedient, either in the consulting room or in bed. He was unable to feel in command of the situation with women; or perhaps we may postulate that for him and others like him, the only way to be in command is to defeat women passively.

Edward:
the need
to placate
women

Edward, like Eamonn, dreamed of marriage to a good woman and longed for children, and decided to seek treatment just one more time, before it was 'too late'. Like Eamonn he had never successfully had intercourse although he had continued, fitfully and with increasing despair and decreasing enthusiasm, to attempt it if and when the opportunity presented with women he liked. He too idealized women and would not dream of trying with casual acquaintances; yet the fact of the women's emotional importance made confident unheeding erection extra difficult. As with others, this was for Edward tied up with the wish to please and placate women, and his sense of the impossibility of achieving it in the face, as he saw it, of his own inadequacy.

Edward soon conveyed his irritation with a previous 'supposedly famous woman sex specialist' who had attempted her own brand of eclectic semi-behavioural encouragement, often highly successful with other patients, but of no help to Edward. This, as he saw it, was because he could not achieve erection with masturbation as instructed and found it meaningless. She had called him, he said, 'a hopeless freak'. Here, however, I was less easily seduced into sharing his sense of outrage, or into a belief that I might do better, so evident was Edward's almost abject need to ingratiate himself with me, his inability to complain directly, and his air of 'pardon me for living'. It looked as though his criticisms of the previous doctor were based on fear — fear of her demands on him and of his own suppressed fury at them. He had fled like a frightened rabbit, not only from this particular therapist, but from any woman who hoped for actual sexual performance from him. His fear of failure, his resentment of their impossible needs, far outweighed his dream of comfortable undemanding love and marriage.

It is interesting that Edward, a distinguished man at his work in academic research, felt terrorized even in a work setting by women, so that an attractive young secretary who forgot he disliked sugar in his coffee seeemed too threatening to be corrected. She might have to bend over him again in her tight sweater; it would be 'too disturbing'. For some months he had been drinking sweetened coffee, despite having to watch his weight since a slight increase in blood pressure. Edward acknowledged that this door-mat feeling in relationship to women was really interfering with his whole life, not just his wish to marry.

Just once, Edward revealed, he had achieved penetration with a girl he much loved. He was only 20 then, and knew little, and had imagined intercourse would be simply a 'blending together' in romantic ecstasy, as in his masturbatory fantasies, and both would love it. He had — but the girl, alas, had not; she had been disappointed at the lack of the thrusting movement that she reasonably expected and that Edward did not know about, or indeed fancy anyway. He had been a newly commissioned second lieutenant in the wartime army at the time, she a canteen worker. He had been brought up by an ailing mother and a forceful grandmother and three 'bossy' elder sisters. His father had been frail and ill from his earliest memory and had died before Edward reached his adolescence, so there was but a shadowy model of how men might deal with these 'powerful' women. He had responded by retreating into his books and had found safe ground in his solitary intellect and in his romantic dreams. He admitted tearfully and indeed sweetly that even with his new-found confidence in his own needs, for which he was able to express his thanks to the doctor calmly and as an equal, the earthy thrusting of basic adult intercourse held no attraction for him.

He was delighted that after some six months of irregular consultations — when he felt like it rather than to fit in with her routine — he had gained confidence and was less threatened by women at work. Several colleagues had remarked how much more fun he seemed to be, and a research paper he had, in self-doubt, left on a dusty shelf, was to be published. He was waking with morning erections regularly (despite his tablets for hypertension, which may sometimes interfere temporarily with erection), and he had masturbated successfully once or twice with his old, romantic fantasies. He felt that after 30 years of 'humiliation' that this was progress; he felt his own man at least and was able to mourn freely with the doctor for his lost dreams.

But he had decided that active sex and marriage were probably not for him, unless he really fell in love 'properly'. He would no longer feel he must shop around frantically in marriage bureaux for anyone who would 'put up with him'. The last session — perhaps one of the most useful — contained some time spent acknowledging his ability, newly acquired, to say metaphorically: 'Thank you very much; but I have all I need from you now, and am not about to keep coming just because you (the doctor) would like more of me.

I feel confident enough to tell you to forget your further hopes for me and know that it can be accepted between us. I can be my own man in relation to you, and say so, and it will not matter.' A good outcome? In terms of sexual performance, it was negligible. In terms of Edward's view of himself as a man, his doctor felt modestly pleased. More importantly, so did Edward.

Part Two

CASE PROFILES ABOUT EXPRESSING NEED

5

The language barrier

Frightened frigidity
Stern mothering
Inner struggles

It has often been said, and in many contexts, that people *The need* need to love themselves before they can love others. It is *to love* my experience that our personal sexuality is an example of *ourselves* this. In Part One a few of the ways in which individuals may find it difficult to enjoy their innermost sexual desires even in the privacy of their own hearts were explored. Feeling free to show these deeper aspects of ourselves openly in the presence of another, and to express them in word and deed, requires an added dimension of confident certainty. There needs to be an inner sense that such vulnerable parts of the self are fit to be seen, acceptable and safe.

Were people merely naked apes, any couple might hope that the first meeting of eyes would trigger mutual discovery. Exploratory courtship would lead on to physical attraction and the warmth of closeness, to steadily heightening arousal and mutual orgasm, as surely as night follows day. Since, however, our species is not just characterized by absence of hair, but described by the suffix 'sapiens', with all the individual complexity of mind and emotion and social sense that we have developed since first standing, literally, upon our own feet, the process is rarely so simple.

To begin with, we are communal creatures. The first meeting of eyes is more likely to be across a crowded room than an empty beach. Social constraints and parental directives may interfere on the one hand. On the other, the wish for mate selection on grounds other than immediate sexual attraction should, if we are sapient enough, enrich our choices.

Despite a relatively new ambience of family mixed bathing in some cultures, the idea that individuals can all revel in physical nakedness without unease is a myth. We tend to blame earlier cultural prohibitions. 'Who told you you were naked?' asked the drab missionary of a Paradise Islander. 'The Mothers' Union, Lord', she is said to have replied. Yet when the clergyman reads his text from Genesis: 'Male and Female created He them', the lady wearing the grand hat in the front pew whispers to her neighbour, 'He should have been ashamed of Himself.' People interpret their own culture, via their own prejudices.

For the less confident individual, it makes little difference whether such uncertainty about personal exposure is labelled 'inhibition', with the hint of contempt that suggests, or, more charitably, 'embarrassment' or 'shyness', the discomfort remains. Yet for confident expression of sexual needs and wishes, people do have to unclothe emotionally, to lay bare those parts of their inner feelings which are normally not for public view, without fear, without shame and without guilt.

Viewed in these terms, the nature of arousal and orgasm takes on a very different light from any study which sees them as a matter of physiological activity or seeks to modify them to the norm of the statistical majority. Confidence about the ways in which sexuality may be used as a means of expression of the feelings of the moment, the individual freedom so to do and the individual difficulties in so doing require personal exploration of how such attitudes may develop or fail to develop in each individual.

Imagine for a moment any everyday sexual encounter in the real world between two reasonably happy, reasonably confident people. Suppose that this is not the first time they have made love together, that they are past the teething troubles and the tentative mutual exploration which every new relationship requires, and that we would not expect either of them to have figured in Part One. Suppose that neither seriously doubts their sexual ability, nor the appropriateness of their wishes for this new (or indeed old) relationship to be sexually expressed – and for it to go well. Suppose too that they know the facts of life and that they find each other attractive and that they are both in agreement. Let us agree before I proceed, that that is assuming much, even for the most confident.

In order to initiate approaches or to respond to hers, to ensure that those approaches lead not only to her arousal but to his own, to move confidently on, to be alert and adaptable to her responses, he must feel some confidence about what is right for him. Furthermore he must feel some certainty that there is no embarrassment within himself about revealing his tastes and preferences to her. If she is free enough to respond with encouragement, whether verbally or non verbally, any marginal doubts of his own will be diminished. If she can however only show what she does not enjoy, by complaint or by flinching or whatever, he will then need to be not too anxious about failing to please her if he is not to lose his own drive. Similarly, he must be not too vulnerable to criticism and must not interpret all comment as such if his confidence is to be maintained. Inner vulnerabilities are not necessarily limited to the matter of purely sexual performance, crucial though that is as a symbol of man's sense of confidence and self-command. We may need to explore, if such crises of confidence arise, why a particular man may be vulnerable. It may be that his sexual difficulty is but a symptom of a more general anxiety about not giving satisfaction, of a more general expectation of criticism and of feeling less than his own man. Much of this may be observed and interpreted usefully in the doctor–patient relationship. Ease of treatment will depend not only upon how far an individual man can use such interpretations, but also to how broad a spectrum of his wishes and activities these doubts apply, and how early and how deeply in his emotional development they may have originated.

Alternatively we may need to explore why a particular woman is thus vulnerable, as her sexual difficulty too may be merely a symptom of more general anxiety about not giving satisfaction, of more general expectation of criticism and of feeling less than her own woman in such circumstances.

It may seem odd that a woman writing towards the end of the 20th century describes a man's uncertainties before a woman's. This is intentional. Woman now have high expectations in their love-lives and they seek help if they are disappointed. Most women appreciate that this increased freedom places its own pressure upon men who are more concerned for women's pleasure than earlier

Womens' expecta- tions: mens' uncertain- ties

generations; and many recognize too, when sexual difficulties arise, how fine is the line between an apparently
welcoming woman and a demanding one in the eyes of an
unconfident man. But not all women perceive that men may
have uncertainties of their own, that they may need
encouragement and reassurance, even help, in their own
right. The notion that all men are naturally more experienced
and better at sex than women can lead to serious
misunderstandings.

Further there is a very common language problem
between the sexes as to 'sex' — often referred to in this
context as 'it' — on the one hand, and 'love' on the other.
Usually, in my experience, it is still the woman who sees
the expression of 'love' in romantic, not overtly sexual terms
— words, flowers, cuddling without arousal — failing to
comprehend that, for her man, his erection is the greatest
compliment he can pay her. Listening with increasing and
uncomprehending dismay to his wife's complaints that he
never said he loved her these days, a Tyneside coal miner
finally spluttered, with obvious tenderness, 'H-away, pet.
I fucks ye, doan't I?

Gerhardt   Many couples I meet are blind to the potential richness
and   of sexuality as an expression of a wide range of emotions,
Greta: the   thereby denying themselves one of the most rewarding
power of   means of human communication. Gerhardt was an inter-
frightened   national businessman whose job involved a high level of
frigidity   decision making and, sometimes, physical danger. During
our consultation he was called to the phone and gave a brisk
and highly impressive answer to a key political question.
He was, on the surface, a man to be reckoned with. Greta,
frail and beautiful, smiled with evident pride. All was not
well with their sex life, however. For Greta, the increasing
strain of waiting with her children in foreign lands, surrounded by servants but far from her parents and always
wondering whether Gerhardt would come home safely, had
resulted in a failure to respond sexually which had led, in
turn, to Gerhardt's relative impotence.

It was clear to me that Greta could only see in Gerhardt
the bold man of power who wanted 'it' as his macho
entitlement. Frustrated by her stressful life, she could not
recognize the vulnerability beneath the commanding veneer,
his need not only for physical satisfaction, but for comfort

and warmth, and an acceptance of the fact that he was sometimes exhausted by the constant pressures of his lonely responsibilities. He, conversely, could see in Greta only a poor little helpless creature. He was blind to the inner strength which might enable her to take care of him sometimes or to her power over him which her frightened frigidity effected. All this was evident to me in the consulting room. However, each time I tried to draw their attention to the destructive effect on them both of her apparent 'weakness', Greta would feel attacked by me just as she did by him, and would melt into tears. This rendered me impotent as a doctor — for I felt as much of a bully as he did. More importantly, the mighty Gerhardt too crumbled before my eyes, anxious and impotent in the face of her weeping. Yet, it was very clear who unwittingly controlled the consultation, and it was not the medical consultant or the man of affairs.

The idea of sexuality as a means of expression can vary enormously — and if the view of what it may be used for is limited, difficulty will be experienced in expressing other things sexually as well. Not only may language barriers arise, as between Gerhardt and Greta, but it will be impossible to show and express sexual feelings freely except in a certain situation, in a certain frame of mind, with the purpose that is felt to be 'right'. Again, the range of variation is infinite, so subtly is every person different from the next. At one extreme, the physiological view might be that the purpose of sexuality is to propagate the species only. How many profound theological arguments begin here, and sadly seem merely to end here. A view of the purpose of human loving which some scholarly churchmen justify as 'spiritual' seems to me a return to the values of the stud farm. For me the truly human advance over this primitive breeding use of sexuality is that we may use it as a means of expression of our whole personality, as a medium of communication of emotions as various as any other — the written or the spoken word, television, painting, music.

This may seem a bit high-minded for many whose love-life is mostly a matter of just muddling along, with mutual tolerance and humour, a few moments of total ecstasy, and a few of disaster. Yet, even those who have been fortunate enough to have some freedom in this respect, whose sexuality is not too conditional, have been unusual if they have never known the magic of a moment clouded by a fleeting sense of the inappropriate. The earthy word, so exciting when we are ourselves in an earthy mood, can be a shocking turn-off if our mood calls for respect or romance or comfort. The truly fortunate are those who are free enough to be sensitive to the mood of the other, to be able to play a different game when required. For those less fortunate, and who seek help, we need again to understand the underlying reasons.

Finding the right 'door' Let us return for a moment to the origins of this work, when we first met our patients in family planning practice. One obvious reason was that in the early days, patients with sexual difficultites did not know where else to go. Nevertheless, even that fact raised questions as to why each person chose that particular agency, for other workers also hear of marital difficulties. Tom Main held that, in very general terms, people find the right 'shop' for their particular problem. When problems are expressed in terms of violence, police and probation officers become involved, and it may be that their clients are unconsciously seeking for some containment and restraint. Bank managers deal with those who worry about money, and divorce lawyers joust on our behalf in disputes over rights and wrongs. Barmaids may hear of those whose wives do not understand them, and neighbours at garden fences hear the grumbles of women when their husbands do not come home. Prostitutes provide the sex that is not available elsewhere, and marriage counsellors, on the whole, hear from couples who see their problem as about the marriage or at least the relationship, rather than as about individual unease. Priests and psychiatrists and family doctors and teachers all have their part to play. How often, for example, will sexual frustration or marital disharmony show itself in the problems of the children failing to thrive educationally, playing truant, or in other behaviour problems? To the Home Office working party on the marriage guidance services of which I was a member, Tom Main's concept of 'many doors', giving people in trouble a wide choice of agencies, was commended. What is vital is not that one be regarded as 'better' than another, but that people should know as they knock what kind of help they will find – and that behind whichever door they choose to enter, they should find the highest integrity and professional skill of the kind they seek.

Most of the patients who came to family planning practice in those days were women, since the male contraceptive methods, the condom and coitus interruptus, did not require medical advice. They were not all, of course, in trouble. As an eminent woman broadcaster once said at a meeting where the emphasis was on sexual problems: 'It was very interesting to be asked about my infancy, but really I only wanted a cap!' We soon recognized that those with some unhappiness on the whole made an apt choice, since a family planning doctor could be expected not only to make a genital examination, but to believe that sex had other purposes than procreation alone. Yet among such patients were many who, so far from needing contraceptive protection, revealed at examination that they had never consummated, that they were *virgo intacta*, though they had refrained from telling us. Why did they need this 'visiting card'?

Much study has been devoted to the need of different patients for an 'acceptable' presenting symptom, not only by the Institute of Psychosexual Medicine, but by the Balint Society, in relation to the much wider variety of problems seen in general practice. Even today many patients find it difficult to come straight out with their real anxiety, if that anxiety seems to them foolish, or incomprehensible, or not what they imagine the doctor wants to hear. If their real worry remains unspoken, they may have to return again and again with other physical pretexts if they feel the doctor is only interested in these. If their doctor is in turn either insensitive or untrained to hear non-verbal communications, not only will the problem remain unsolved and their despair increased, but they run into danger of feeling, and indeed appearing to the doctor as a nuisance and a 'neurotic'. The hope of accurate diagnosis and help only recedes further. A doctor who only recognizes physical ailments may then order more and more complex investigations or surgery to exclude physical illness, and thus only reinforce patients' fears of foolishness or abnormality, missing the diagnosis entirely.

It is often easier in some cultures for a man to complain of 'weakness' than of impotence. In ordinary conversation we do not call our nuisances a 'headache' for nothing. It would be inaccurate to suggest that the language of the *The language of symptoms* presenting symptom is always linked with the nature of the psychosomatic anxiety. It is interesting, however, how often it turns out to be the case. Women complaining of 'irritation', for example, will need careful checking for infections and allergies; but if no physical disease is found, it is significant that often the discovery of irritation emotionally will help to remove the symptom. The last time I was consulted by someone in that situation, her adolescent daughter's untidiness seemed to be the source. More precisely, the patient's feelings about the dirty tights in the washbasin and the cigarette ash in the unmade bed were irritating. Although she loved the girl dearly, she felt it was about time that her daughter looked after her own personal hygiene. There was also a less conscious envy, not only of the girl's emerging sexuality but of her ability to be happy-go-lucky and 'sluttish' without shame.

Helped to see this, and to recognize that she was entitled to her 'irritation', my patient felt free to convert less into her physical symptom. She was also able to speak firmly with her daughter, woman-to-woman, avoiding the alternating frustration and temperamental outbursts when the control snapped, which had been seriously endangering the mother and daughter communication.

Another symptom which may often have similar origins is neck pain. Osteopaths and acupuncturists, not to mention orthopaedic surgeons and physiotherapists, know how common this is, and how difficult it is to treat satisfactorily, particularly when no specific organic lesion can be detected. A woman whose 'pain in the neck' was her bossy but ailing mother-in-law had converted her own feelings of suppressed and guilty rage towards her. A man who was suppressing resentment of his wife's frigidity since the birth of a damaged child was ashamed at acknowledging negative feelings towards someone whom he could not legitimately blame and whom he felt he ought to be able to protect and cherish. That gave him, literally, a 'pain in the neck'.

Psychosomatic symptoms should not imply that the symptoms are imaginary or that the patient is malingering. Unrelieved tension leads to muscular and neurological tension. No-one whose flesh has 'crept' or who has suffered 'goose-pimples' at the sight of a spider or the finding of half a maggot in a salad, can doubt that the skin is affected by emotional feeling, to cite but one body symptom.

Even today, when counselling services abound and sexual pleasure and sex therapy are widely accepted as subjects for public debate, many men and women still find it impossible to walk into a clinic or doctor's surgery and say openly, 'My love-life is disappointing. Please help me.' Those words are hard to say.

A distinguished agony columnist once attacked an audience of family doctors. Were they doing their job properly, she implied, she would not have her yearly case-load of 50 000 letters. She had a point, of course: but not every doctor has the time, the training or the sensitivity for psychosexual medicine. I believe patients who are courageous enough to go to the surgery with a respectable 'visiting card', perhaps leaving again with the true problem unexpressed, are the merest tip of an iceberg. It may well be that those who contact the agony columnist include many who can only write, secretly and anonymously, from the privacy of their rooms, unable to bring themselves out to professional consultation even if a name or place has been suggested to them. And this is, I propose, to be attributed not so much to the lack of facilities for help, but rather to the individual's shyness and, particularly for men, to the inner imperative to cope unaided. They fear the exposure not only of their sexuality but of their need to complain and seek help.

A variety of defences are built against these inner vulnerabilities, and the lack of confidence to overcome them may be little to do with what we see as 'sexual', in the sense of adult erotic performance. Yet for an individual, the sense of what needs to be concealed will increasingly intrude upon sexual confidence if the view of the purpose of sex is rigidly limited.

Rachel had always been sexually shy and had never dared, never even considered thinking about what might be more pleasurable for her in a rather routine married life with a husband who, she readily admitted, had never lacked either sexual enthusiasm or a wish to make it good for her. Her 'visiting card' was a request for a routine smear — she wondered 'whether she was near the change'. As she had no symptoms whatsoever and was only about forty, this was unlikely, so it was necessary to ask her whether there was something else worrying her. Only then did her eyes fill with tears and the story of sexual disappointment emerged. In her choice of presentation or 'visiting card' there had already been some hints. She had told me that her son had just celebrated his Bar Mitzvah before mentioning her own problems. Rachel, an Orthodox Jewess, set herself standards of mothering and had put those standards higher on her lists of priorities than sexual pleasure. She then offered hints of anxiety about ageing. Perhaps her son's emergent manhood reminded her that time was running on, and in her duty to home and family, the young girl in her had been lost. Or perhaps, like so many others, she felt that, having achieved her mothering goal, she might at last seek pleasure for herself.

Rachel was able to elaborate on all these threads and felt that all had some reality for her. She became thoughtful about her previous inability to think of her sexual life in terms other than marital duty — both for her husband and for childbearing. She could not remember how she dreamed it would be in her youth, but she did remember that she had dreamed. On her return later she said she had felt free to convey something of her wishes to her husband for the first time ever. 'Crazy,' she said, 'but I was really frightened that it would offend him after all this time — that he would think me complaining, or forward, or I don't know what. But would you believe,' she went on, 'I didn't actually have to *say* anything, after I'd lain awake rehearsing; I just dared to move a bit, and he was delighted.'

As she was about to leave she said shyly, 'He's outside actually, would you like to meet him?' I was quite surprised at Abe, for from her description he had sounded rather authoritarian. In fact, he revealed that he had his own fears that his idealized wife would see his sexual approaches as rough, uncouth and beneath her. 'My life,' he said, blushing rosily, 'I felt she was interested for the first time ever . . . I thought she had just put up with me all these years. Magic, I call it.' They left, chuckling.

Clearly there was nothing very deep-seated in Rachel's shyness about expressing her personal needs, and her sexuality had been easily revived by the observation that her physical complaint could not be quite what it seemed. In response to an accurate and professional observation, she felt entitled to speak of her sexual disappointment. It was enough, apparently, for her and Abe to move forward with increased confidence. Yet before we leave them, do you know what she actually liked? I don't! It is not, of course, our business . . . and if Abe does, from some subtle more active movement, we may be thankful. Many husbands would need more positive spelling out before they could hope to get their foreplay right for such a shy woman. Those who are less easily freed than Rachel may, in their silence, make it impossible for even the most experienced lover to guess what they might enjoy.

Behavioural encouragement to touch, explore, express preference without challenge, can of course be most helpful to many people like Rachel and Abe. To be ordered by an authoritative and respectable therapist to spend regular time and energy and thought on pure pleasure is to reinforce a sense of entitlement forcefully and often fruitfully. However, we may ask ourselves why an individual needs it so, and why, if it happens, they resent or resist it. Interestingly, to be told to pull oneself together or to be lectured to as a learner may for some feel just like this, in contrast to the kind of listening therapy which allows patients their own pace and respects their own need to be guarded. Without help, however, our defences, being unwitting, may make of us our own worst enemies if we are unaware in our fear how awkward we appear to others.

Ruth was also Jewish, though I have met many like both *Ruth:* her and Rachel who were not. Only in her late twenties, *inner* Ruth was in no need of pretexts. She asked for referral to *struggles* a specialist quite soon after her marriage, since, as her male doctor's letter said, 'Her husband was unable to arouse her.' So even before I had met Ruth I know that at least she was able to feel entitled to some arousal and demand it. Yet, it was an odd way to put it, as though her arousal was seen as her husband's responsibility. Perhaps this was her doctor's view. When Ruth, a bright young businesswoman, arrived, she insisted forcefully that she herself did see it that way, that her husband was failing her in some way and she was pretty fed up with not getting her due. I felt my hackles rising, and found myself observing that another might put it that it was she who could not allow herself to be aroused by him. Were we here, I asked, to apportion blame or rather to help with difficulty?

Now these interpretations were useful and, as it proved, accurate, but I was aware as I made them that they were coming from me in a pretty attacking tone of voice. Why? I am normally quite good-natured — interested in and even fond of my patients. Had I got out of bed the wrong side, or was it something Ruth was provoking in me? Ruth did blink at the idea that she might have some part to play but came back fighting with another anti-men attack assuming that I, as an intelligent career woman, knowing, as she put it contemptuously, what 'these men are all like', would agree with her. Well, men are not all alike any more than women or Jews or any other group are all alike, and, for my part, I find many of them quite delightful! And here I was, in danger of arguing with a girl in trouble whom I'd hardly met.

It soon became possible to notice and share with Ruth that my reaction provided a clue to the way in which she presented herself to the outside world: tough, resentful, waspish, not making it easy for me to see her needs or respond to them caringly. Maybe it was equally difficult for her husband to understand her needs. I wondered why she needed this outward defensiveness? So began a number of conversations which strayed often from the mere sexual difficulty to discussions about Ruth's equivalent of the Sleeping Beauty's 'thicket'; about the defences she had built around her against fear of emotional hurt should she let down her guard, not only in bed but in other kinds of trusting relationships too. People find various defences against rejection or vulnerability. Ruth's style was to become combative against her husband. We could soon agree together that the really important fight was within herself, not so much with her husband as with her needy feelings for him.

Some of her feelings and defences were very like those of another myth which Balint used to describe some women with consummation difficulties, namely that of Brunhilde [6]. She saw her sexuality as something to be fought for: only the man who overcame her in physical combat could possess her. In my experience, many women see their desires and the purpose of their sexuality in this way — as a matter of resisting the man as instigator until she is overcome. This element in us may be so strong, or so fear- or guilt-ridden, that we fight not only the man but these frightening desires within us with such vigour that we suppress them entirely, and with them, regrettably, our capacity for sexual excitement. For Ruth and Brunhilde, this inner struggle can be destructive not only to their own wishes to be swept off their feet, but to the confidence of the men who would wish to, if they could let them. It is customary to refer to this idea as the 'rape wish'. For my part, I find it hard to believe than any woman consciously desires or invites 'rape', but if we speak instead of the excitement of being carried away in delight in spite of ourselves, it may sound less destructive. As every sexually confident woman knows, the voluntarily abandoning of defences can, when the mood is right, be a triumphant experience.

It is a widespread misapprehension that the theory of psychoanalysis implies apportioning blame to awkward parents or circumstances. Some of us have luckier starts than others, and some experience such devastating and self-evident trauma that we cannot be expected to emerge emotionally unscathed. However, in psychosexual medicine at least, it is the individual's ways of responding to and coping with their outside world *as it is* which we try to help them understand and perhaps review.

Ruth's vision of her own development and the important people around her was that she was happy and much loved. Her father, she felt, adored her no matter what. 'I could do no wrong with him. He used to say the sun shone out of my eyes . . . it was our joke.' Nor did her mother, as she saw it, have any resentment of this. They both showed great pride in her attractiveness to boys — who, in her mother's expression, were 'like moths round a candle' — as well as in her academic achievements. Yet as our talks went on, it became clear that her mother seemed the powerful one in the family and that her father's unquestioning devotion to them both somehow diminished him in their eyes. Indeed, Ruth had reached the stage where she could blurt out tearfully, in talking about her husband: 'I seem to be turning into a real old Yiddisher Mama . . . I've always been terrified of that', and then at once, in horror, 'What am I saying? My mother really isn't like that at all. She's been wonderful to me. What am I saying?'

Without asking any direct questions, I was interested to notice that this remark reminded Ruth of some family folklore. That she should 'associate' in this way suggested that the history, or her view of it, was relevant to the problem at hand. Ruth had known none of her grandparents, but remembered being told many stories about them. Her father's family lived in New York. Her own father's modestly successful business did not sound on her lips to be quite in the same league as the company-lawyer brother who had succeeded to her grandfather's practice. Ruth's mother had been sent on holiday to France in the 1930s with her little brother and an aunt and had never returned to their home in Germany. The rest of the family had perished in the gas chambers.

Parents intern- alized as models   What relevance to Ruth's defensive toughness can we find here? I elaborate because unlike some who find their own ways in rebellion against some real or perceived parental value systems, Ruth seemed instead to have learned from her parents by internalizing them as models. We can see clearly why her parents might well be as she saw them. Ruth's mother, after all, had to learn to cope emotionally when very young, to survive. Nor is it surprising that her father had, as a loving, easygoing man, dealt with the highly competitive rivalries of a tough and successful family by making his own comfortable way (at a safe distance), not wanting such demanding standards to taint his own family and by making sure they all felt loved as they were, without the need for diplomas or commercial acumen. This had come across to Ruth as, on the one hand, the need for women to be tough survivors, and on the other that these men, who adored you regardless, were somehow to be thought less of for it.

It is hard to analyse and to document how Ruth, and many others like her, could feel less defensive, could find her own image of safe womanhood and be able to trust it to her man, simply by being able to 'rabbit on', as she described it, for a few sessions with me. It must be apparent from this account that I was unable to make any precise and sophisticated interpretations, yet it somehow became clear both to her and to me that these images had played their part in her difficulty in showing the less defensive, more dependent aspects of her personality. Their love-life improved. She had never had difficulty with orgasm itself, particularly by clitoral stimulation (which is, in a sense, a less 'abandoned' experience than climax within intercourse), but their preliminaries had been something of a mutual coaching session, even a battleground. Ruth forgot, eventually, why she had first attended. Do you remember? It was ostensibly because her husband, whom I never met, was no good, and was failing to arouse her! But now Ruth was not only able to allow herself to be aroused by him by, as she said, 'his just being there', but to enjoy showing her own pleasure to him without restraint, and to trust herself to him without hectoring.

I subsequently received a card announcing the arrival of Ruth's first son. Lest it seem that she had somehow been brainwashed into feeling that domesticity was a higher calling, or had lost her independent career-girl spark in her new-found warmth towards her husband, I can issue a confident denial. Indeed, soon after their marriage had become easier, both Ruth and her husband had achieved promotions in their separate jobs. Often a man whose confidence is diminished either by his own sexual difficulty or his wife's unresponsiveness, burgeons forth in other ways when that problem is solved. That women too find their confidence improved in other ways — competitive and professional ways sometimes — by feeling easier with themselves sexually, may seem harder to accept, especially for those who see these aspects of their lives as incompatible with their notions of femininity. However in clinical practice, I have often found it to be the case.

We begin to see these matters as less to do with trusting or failing to trust the opposite sex, than with being better able to trust oneself — and one's own instincts and deepest feelings. It is thus that real freedom may be found to relate to the other, without internal doubts, and by making a conscious choice.

6

Letting go

Disciplined desire
Sex for procreation
A feared view of womanhood
Controlled violence and ejaculation
An absent patient

Orgasm has always seemed to me to be a particularly unattractive word which completely fails to convey the beauty of the experience it describes. Perhaps it is the hint of 'orgy' which feels to me inappropriate to such an intimate matter, or perhaps it is hearing patients often call it in error 'organism', which suggests the idea that it is something that happens to triffids. Is 'climax' better? The comparison with the closing moments of Beethoven's Ninth Symphony or with athletes breasting a tape seems to approach the experience.

That so many words evolve to describe universal experience suggest how variously individuals view it. To 'come' when used as 'come together' has an accurate simplicity but many use 'come' as a synonym for emission, referring to 'his come'. Since women rarely produce anything comparable, this hints at one-sidedness and moves away from the idea of mutuality. 'Making it' seems to me to be an even less satisfactory euphemism. In England at least we use 'I made it' or 'I just made it' for last-minute feats such as catching a train or surviving a dangerous hazard, the implications being that of a daunting struggle.

It is impossible to avoid the essential humour, the ludicrousness, of the public description of an act which can be so precious for those involved in it. A television critic wrote that a tight head shot (of the woman) must be intended to indicate either that she is having an orgasm, or that she has accidentally stuck a toe into a light socket, and goes on to describe her partner in passion as appearing to have been bitten on the behind by a large dog. But this is the observer's problem . . .

Some therapists believe that to be able to watch blue movies without flinching, or to discuss one's masturbatory habits in groups, helps to overcome sexual shyness in private. It is not my experience that it achieves any more than the ability to be a more comfortable voyeur.

In a debate about what was appropriate for family viewing, a friend who is a thoroughly uninhibited and sophisticated woman in her own sexuality in private admitted her discomfort at watching explicit lovemaking in the cinema, particularly in the company of friends. Asked if she objected to kids making love in the park, when perhaps they had nowhere else to go, she replied, 'No. There's nothing more delicious than making love in the open air. But I'd not', she went on, 'settle down with a bag of peanuts to watch. And I hope no-one would queue up with their hot-dogs and choc-ices to watch me!'

Is it appropriate that I should reveal some of my own feelings as a woman in a book which is primarily intended to convey some of my professional insights? Appropriate or not, it seems to me inescapable. Professionals who use the language of technology, describing the disappointment of intense excitement without completion as 'orgasmic dysfunction' seem to me to be asserting their own values in much this way. This is how they see it, as a matter of the mechanical failure of a bodily function. My defence is that as a woman I have my own wishes and disappointment, my own preferences and delights. As a doctor I must remember that these are personal. Only when personal feelings lead to personal distress does 'treatment', become relevant, and that 'treatment' must be geared to the wishes of the individual for change, not to my, or anyone else's, vision of a norm.

Is orgasm really necessary? A woman psychoanalyst of great distinction states firmly in her admirable lecture on female sexuality that it is not. In a sense, I agree with her. If we see it as a performance-orientated goal, as a *sine qua non* of satisfactory lovemaking, then we not only miss the potential richness of all the other rewarding aspects of making 'love' rather than 'it', but in so doing make a rod for our own backs. For orgasm itself is not something that can be achieved by voluntary effort, even though we may strive to some extent for the necessary arousal to make it possible. Ultimately, it is something we can only let happen. It is in individual difficulty with that concept, with daring to abandon conscious control and let something happen to us, that most problems with climax occur, for men and women alike.

Perhaps the people whom the analyst meets, who are exploring their whole personalities in detail, may find any such goal expectation an irrelevance. But for the people I meet, who are unable to complete their lovemaking in climax and who feel that they are missing something, it certainly does matter deeply. Nor is the sex difference as clear-cut as many believe. The idea that the woman as the receiver, the responder, can be equally rewarding to her man whether she enjoys that final abandonment or not, may be true for many but not for all. Nor is it always the woman who complains greedily for herself. Many men feel themselves a failure should their woman be left unfulfilled in this way. Both sexes may feel that without a woman's climax an intangible but deep and important emotional part of herself is held back, and women whose husbands are unable to ejaculate are, similarly, not always dissatisfied simply because they want babies. Many feel that their man is somehow holding back a bit of his unguarded deepest emotional self. The often multiple orgasms they can achieve with a lover who can struggle on without ejaculation indefinitely are no substitute for this feeling of total sharing and abandonment . . . the blurring of the edges of self, the feeling of becoming for a moment the completely at one 'two-backed beast'. It can matter even for those who, unselfishly as they would see it, do not complain, for fear of hurting the other, or for some sense of lack of entitlement in themselves. I meet many for whom it matters a lot, but for whom the problem is not so much that as the fact that they have difficulty in acknowledging that it matters — to their partners or even to themselves.

Paul and Pamela and Doris and Dafydd had a lot in common: most of all they were all good, uncomplaining people. This time I shall tell two stories when either might serve to illustrate a point, because although their social backgrounds were very different, they show equally the burdens of setting high standards for ourselves.

Paul and Pamela became engaged at the 'right' age, delighting their parents who were lifelong friends in the same 'county' set. Both had been privately educated, with no great trauma about their boarding schools. Pamela enjoyed finishing school in Switzerland, became a fine skier and was fluent in French. She would have liked to earn her living — 'at something useful, like say doing something in French Africa with UNICEF', but she met Paul first and fell in love. He was a good cricketer who loved the outdoor life, and he would have liked to have been a farmer, but there was no prospect of that kind of capital being available to him. The long grind to qualify as a chartered accountant was tough for one who hated maths and hated commuting to a dirty city even more. He achieved it by sheer hard work, with little time for fun or for playing the field with girls. But he met Pamela at a cricket house-party and fell in love in his turn, and at their charming country wedding they were both virgins still, despite the intensity of their passion and their romantic dreams. They had been brought up with the idea that to wait was not only safer, but implied positive respect.

Because they had disciplined their desires, neither found it easy to release control, to abandon themselves primitively and wildly to sexuality, just because the marriage, as it said in the social columns, had taken place. Paul was a bit quick and clumsy to begin with, and Pamela, though she found intercourse 'wildly exciting', could not quite reach orgasm in these circumstances. Being good-natured and shy, she did not dare to complain about how frustrated she felt, or to suggest ways in which Paul might have helped. Because Paul was nice, he tried hard, thus being under extra pressure to 'succeed', wanting to please without knowing quite how. After a bit he became able to prolong his erections, and Pamela conceded that she could no longer account for her inability to let go to full enjoyment in terms of his failure as a lover. She was aware that in the face of the great disappointment of regularly nearly reaching orgasm and being let down, it became harder to allow such intense arousal. Thus the likelihood of improvement, even when he could maintain long erection, diminished. She said, 'it was as though I knew I couldn't whatever he did.' Paul's disappointment in failing, as he saw it, to give her equal joy to his own, naturally reduced his eagerness. Less nice people

Paul and Pamela: desire disciplined

might have seen it differently. Both heard the other's lessening confidence negatively. He began to feel his approaches were a nuisance to her. She felt she must please him, and rather than risk his knowing of another failure to orgasm, began to fake it. Later she started to think of other things: first, of him and his pleasure; then of the babies they wanted and had; later still of the shopping-list, if not actually of England!

Paul did not, as his love-life with the woman he loved and desired became less and less rewarding, take his secretary as his mistress, or stay longer and longer at the cricket club drinking with the chaps. He loved his children and made of his marriage a friendship. Nor did Pamela seek a lover or take to her chaise longue and complain. She did good works and loved her children and made of her marriage a friendship.

Rage turned inwards When I met them their children were grown, Paul's hair was thinning; his face was strained; he had anti-acid tablets in his briefcase and his recent director's check-up had revealed a marginal rise in blood pressure. Pamela was having migraine when she was on the pill but heavy periods (menorrhagia) without it, and was booked for a hysterectomy. It was good, both agreed, that they had still such a warm relationship, but now that the children had left home, their lives seemed hollow. Both could make the other feel like a dear old soul, a reliable companion. Neither could make the other feel, as we all need to be made to feel sometimes, irresistible! And since both remained even now good nice people, neither could rage, overtly and without guilt, at each other, or at the gods, for their disappointments and lost dreams. Each raged, as far as they could at all, at themselves, bottling up tensions into physical symptoms. It is rarely the businessman who scoots off to the Bahamas with his mistress and the loot who gets ulcers or raised blood pressure. More often it is the one who, like Paul, keeps trying responsibly, internalizing his stresses and dissatisfactions.

Nor is the woman who can more easily let free her negative feelings — or disappointment and resentment and blaming — without guilt, as likely to turn these inward to cause psychosomatic stress symptoms. She may be less pleasant company, nagging or ranting or being sorry for herself, but her own inner tensions may be thus relieved. In an early study about women who were capable of intense arousal but unable to 'let it go' to orgasm, menorrhagia was found to be quite common. Of course, there are many serious and wholly physical reasons for this heavy menstrual bleeding which must be investigated and treated, just as there are for headaches and high blood pressure and ulcers. But stress and pelvic congestion do not help. Tom Main postulated that these women who were regularly frustrated but who bottled up their resentments were meno-'raging' at something inside themselves. Hormones and/or surgery were often necessary, but if they were helped to feel easier about their need to 'rage', their bleeding was sometimes reduced also. Discussing this idea once in a television interview I coined the phrase 'the Geordie Stevenson syndrome'. Too late I found myself in error — James Watt was the man I had in mind! But my thinking about the effects of bottled-up tension upon the health of 'nice' or 'good' people held. You will recall that it was not, Watt noticed, merely the inner boiling steam which provided the surging power that was to tow trains full of people from Stockton to Darlington, and later from Inverness to London and from the Atlantic to the Pacific. It was keeping the lid pressed down on the kettle.

Doris and Dafydd were truly poor when I met them. They had come to London from the South Wales valley which was family home for them both in the hope of better job prospects. Doris had found work as a supply teacher but Dafydd's morale was low, since he could only find poorly paid, casual, unskilled labour. He had started life as an apprentice in the highly skilled and dangerous world of the steel-works. His vision of his lack of achievement, not only in relation to his wife's 'women's work' in paying their small mortgage, robbing him of his status as provider, but, in relation to the tough proud skills of father and uncles and grandfathers before them, was little helped by the knowledge that in a time of general recession this was a poor reflection of his own abilities. A man more at ease with his aggression might have released some of his 'impotent' rage in protest at the foundry gates. Dafydd, like Paul, kept struggling peaceably to find his own independence in impossible circumstances.

Doris and Dafydd: sex for procreation

Though not tall, Dafydd was a muscular man with bright blue eyes and a shock of black curly hair. He had played fly-half for a team where you have to be very tough to play fly-half, in that world of the heart of Rugby Union, where 14–stone coal-miners hurtle down upon one another, breaking from the back row of the scrum at high speed. He had too, Doris told me, a grand baritone voice, and from the twinkle in his eye I could guess this was employed not only in the chapel choir but in rugby songs after the match.

I met them because, although they could not really afford it and had been waiting in the hope that their lot might improve, both longed for children and Doris was now 30. There was no apparent physical reason for their failure so far to conceive, and they both knew in their hearts it was because they no longer often made love spontaneously; they had to make a special effort to do so at mid-month. Both had come to feel shy, awkward and embarrassed about this, Dafydd sometimes failing to ejaculate and feeling wanted only for the potential child. Doris, it at once emerged, had never reached orgasm or indeed any sense of pleasure or arousal from intercourse. They had found it most enjoyable for her to be brought to climax by clitoral petting first, after which Dafydd would enter and reach his own climax. So they could hardly have been considered to have a sexual problem, until intercourse 'to order' for conception had coincided with a life situation in which Dafydd's sense of fun and lionhood was under pressure also.

It would have been easy to fasten upon his inadequacies, for being a nice man he felt that the burden of responsibility was upon him. But brief discussion of how the carefree rugger player, the promising apprentice, the 'bit of a lad' with the girls, and all the dreams of a confident future as his own master had become lost, seemed enough for him to perk up, not only in morale but sexually too, by their second visit. So it was necessary to notice that Doris merited some concern also: that were she more able eagerly to enjoy intercourse for its own sake, the odds on so doing at the fertile time might be greatly increased. As so often with any couple who agree that sex and its success or failure are the man's responsibility and that climax for the girl is something that must be 'given to her' rather than achieved for herself, it would have been easy to neglect her personal needs and responsibility in treatment. She reflected this in the consultation, leaving the talking to Dafydd, nodding wisely and even admiringly as he spoke of the man he once was, but amazed if the doctor drew attention to her own passivity and apparent acceptance that there was nothing she could do to help.

Doris, it then emerged, had reasons why she had been unable to enjoy the sensation of intercourse, or believe in it as a source of pleasure in its own right. Her upbringing had been 'chapel' like Dafydd's, but in a family not only more strict and protective sexually to its girls, but with a strongly puritanical work ethic also. The idea that sex was primarily for the procreation of children and that the pleasure aspect was really for the men was not unusual in such a family. Girls were to say no until they were married, when they were to say yes; but the fact that they might actually want it, long for it, be excited by it, was prohibited.

Thus when Doris found the usual intense sexual desires stirring within her at adolesence, they made her feel disturbed and guilty. Like most women, she discovered the masturbatory potential of her clitoris and enjoyed it furtively, but she did not relate these good climactic sensations to the internal muscular movements, imagining that intercourse would be for the man, and that her pleasure would remain in the clitoral satisfaction she knew. The idea that intercourse might have good sensations of its own, that the vagina was not a hidden, passive 'don't touch' department for the exodus of periods and babies, but an organ of loving, was amazing to her. On the couch the doctor could show her than even in the non-erotic situation of clinical examination, she could feel the pressure of the doctor's fingers inside, and that there were pressure nerve endings there which could be affected by tightening and relaxing the pelvic floor muscles. Doris was delighted not only that this was something new to her, but that it was something she could do for herself – and that she had some entitlement to act positively in the quest for enjoyment.

On their return Doris told how she had experienced quite intense sensation during intercourse for the first time. 'Lovely, it was,' she said, 'so I thought to myself, now, I must try harder . . . and I lost it.' Encouraging Doris to feel free to own her own body and its desires had certainly helped. But the bit of Doris that had learned to control such desires throughout her adolescence had not been helped by being given different instructions by another authority figure. At the point of impending orgasm, fearful of losing control of these turbulent feelings, Doris had automatically reverted to her control system, consciously 'working at it'. She could agree with the doctor that she had instantly turned back into a 'good' woman, effortfully striving, instead of being able to let feeling flood through her. By the third visit she had enjoyed intercourse to the full for the first time in her life. They had made love often and there was no sign of Dafydd's failure of ejaculation. Neither could remember, as they laughingly had to consult a diary, where Doris had been in her cycle; but seven-pound Gareth arrived not much more than nine months later!

Acts of I have always been aware, even in writing brief technical
faith articles for professional readership, how hard it is to convey firm concepts about such dynamic intangibles as human feeling. I have often puzzled about the language problem that interferes between people of different disciplines in their quests for what must ultimately be the same truths, if truths they be, by definition. Perhaps the analysts' view of the 'psyche' and the biblical 'soul' are not so much translations of each other as the same thing. The more we puzzle over the astronomers' black holes and big bangs and the more we learn of Darwin's theory of evolution, the more the first chapter of Genesis and other creation myths seem not so much mumbo-jumbo as a poetic interpretation of a similar idea. It is fascinating how readily we accept the number of light years to the planets and the structure of the atom, even that two and two make four, without noticing that to do so is basically an act of faith. But to comprehend that there is an unconscious mind about which there is a tested body of knowledge does not seem widely possible yet. We all think ourselves amateur psychologists, knowing what we can know of ourselves — which excludes, of course, by definition, the unconscious.

In trying to communicate that which, as they say about the peace of God, 'passeth all understanding' in the Christian tradition and the equivalent in others, maybe the best we can do is simply to acknowledge that if we feel we have defined these indefinables, then we have it wrong. And so it is with the emotions of individuals and their relationships, since in every moment they change, and are changed by the moment. This is so with their treatment and with the therapist's training experience. In training and in treatment and in all relationships, especially in love, the raising of an eyebrow, the drawing of a breath, the flinching of a muscle, can mean that nothing is ever quite the same again. It is impossible to conceptualize in ways that 'science', technology or statistics can tolerate. To do so is to try to put a quart into a pint pot (or a litre into a half-litre jug). To bear this as a therapist is hard; to bear it as a patient in trouble is perhaps harder. We long to know where our feelings will lead us, the future of our relationships. Those who can tolerate life's uncertainties without too much need for that kind of assurance are less likely to need didactic assurance from others.

'Acts of faith' is not a bad description of some aspects of this work. For doctors (which may of course be translated as 'teachers') to dare to open their minds and their hard-won skills to the world of uncertainty, or eclecticism, of not knowing what is best for patients, is hard. Balint referred to the doctor's 'apostolic function' [1]. Anyone in the 'caring' or teaching professions has to some extent an authority role. Our patients need it in us to some degree in order to be able to trust themselves to us, but if that is all they get, they will not be helped in finding their own paths. But not all doctors or other therapists — or indeed parents — can be expected to be capable of such an act of faith, or dare to expose themselves to such an abandonment of their certainties as to be quiet and listen and wonder.

Similarly, not every patient can dare to so abandon their defensive certainties as to be able to trust their imagination to a therapist who will only puzzle with them, providing no clever answers. Some people will not only need, but will only be able to use, a different kind of treatment, with rules to be followed and instructions to be obeyed.

I have come to believe that for some people, like Pamela and Doris, to allow orgasm, that most 'abandoned' and out-of-control experience, may be compared with an act of faith at a much simpler level. I have compared it with different patients to learning to swim, to ski or to ride a bicycle. Each of these can be learned in theory, but each finally requires an act of confidence. You have, when the moment comes, to believe the water will hold you up, that throwing your weight away from the hill does work, and that when Daddy lets go of the saddle, pedalling will take you on,

Acts of confidence

unsupported. I used to think that this letting go in trust was mostly a matter for women. I now believe, however, that for men who find difficulty in ejaculating something similar applies. It must relate partly to an almost physical sense of danger of being out of control. Since I can swim and ski and ride a bicycle, perhaps a better illustration for me would be, say, rugger or rock-climbing. It appears more dangerous to tackle low; to sway out on a rope would be beyond my courage. Yet I am assured that you are less likely to be injured if you have your man by the ankles than by his hips; and that at a sheer thousand feet, balance really is all! Your life may depend on it.

Where psychosexual understanding may help is in identifying the fear of what may happen when you are 'out of control' in orgasm. Sometimes these are quite simple things, like making a fool of yourself, or crying out, or passing wind. But as Alfred Hitchcock well knew, the fear of the unknown is the worst fear of all.

Just as it may be simple, by respecting a patient's defences, to get in touch with an individual fear or phantasy about penetration at the moment of genital examination, so a comparable approach may reveal what is feared by a particular patient about being out of control in orgasm. The 'uncontrolled outburst' — a vivid phrase for male orgasm I owe a friend and colleague — rarely seems as daunting when shared as an idea in the cool light of day and in the safety of the consulting room. For some, however, it may be much more difficult. Even for those whose need to keep control has emerged in an otherwise confident adolescent, the defences may have become so important to their sense of comfortable self that it is hard to feel they can be abandoned without also abandoning much of the face that has come to be presented to the world, and which the world seems to value.

Belinda: feared view of woman-hood
Belinda was a beautiful and talented girl whose difficulties with orgasm had already led to the breakdown of an early marriage to a childhood sweetheart. I worked with her in her despair in those days, but can claim no credit for her present happiness with another. Her story gives a vivid illustration of how the defences some of us are forced to acquire may, in the praise they invite and receive, become self-fulfilling. Her background was Liverpool-Irish — poor

and rough. The eldest of the large family of a struggling downtrodden mother and a father prone to drunkenness and violence, she had responsibilities beyond her years and a grim vision of adulthood and marriage. One would hardly expect her mother to have conveyed an idealistic view of the beauty of sex. Confusion about parental sex and violence in an overcrowded back-to-back slum dwelling, with bedrooms and even beds shared, was inevitable. Belinda was highly intelligent and, though fond of both her parents, longed to escape. The need to cope with the little ones during her mother's frequent ill-health, and the duty to scrub the floors after the father's vomiting, was taken in her stride. Eventually Belinda did get away as she won a local beauty contest which was followed by modelling contracts and acting offers. She became a 'star', was able to send money home, 'and they all lived happily ever after' . . . For Belinda, however, the very image that won her public acclaim, the fresh-faced asexual snow-white child princess, was her defence against the sordid baby-machine view of womanhood that she most feared. It was, not surprisingly, difficult for her to abandon this sexually, to risk in love the dark view of what she as a woman might become if she was not careful. Thankfully, her story did have, eventually, a happy ending. She has a good marriage and children and is a star still, but no longer cast in idealized and unreal roles of young, unreachable women.

Bill, a police officer, had never been able to ejaculate — *Bill:* not even , as far as he knew, in sleep. Though he was able *violence* to give his wife multiple orgasms by remaining erect for long *and* periods inside her, when a baby was wanted they were in *ejacula-* trouble. His wife had had many attempts at artificial *tion* insemination by a number of donors without success, for *controlled* Bill was unable even to produce a semen specimen by masturbation. Many men however who are otherwise confident do find that difficult. To produce a specimen in a clinical setting is often impossible especially if it is associated with the fear that the product may be inadequate. Even more interestingly, some men who have had vasectomies and are thus, rationally, only too eager to be found sperm-free and therefore sexually free, may find it difficult, almost as if, as one man put it, 'a bit of me didn't want to know my fertility was over'.

In this case, Bill's marriage was in some danger; both were in despair. Bill was, in his own world, also something of a star. As a young man he had been a boxer and the local champion, who was much admired for his clean style and his consummate sportsmanship in a potentially dirty game. As an idealist and a loving son and brother, he put women on a pedestal, because, it seemed, he had been the strongest member of a family in which father and brothers were less physically able. He felt he had to take responsibility for his mother, who, not surprisingly, was very proud of her athletic son. It was clear from his attitude to me, another older woman, that this attractive man, a gentle giant in a man's world, had no idea that he had any negative and aggressive feelings towards women. Nor was I able to put him in touch with those feelings, for when I felt them coming across to me he could only deny them politely. Indeed the few times my interpretations did seem to get close, he was clearly terrified of them and decided against further consultations.

But how strange, you may say, that a man so uneasy about his aggressive impulses should triumph in such an aggressive sport. Like Leroy (Chapter 4), Bill did not see it this way. He saw his skills in terms of controlling his violence; the men he fought with were his equals. Had he ever thrown a punch in anger he would have felt such shame that he would have never fought again. It was very difficult for Bill to believe that to let himself go with a woman was not to let loose dangerous impulses. His aggression towards me was totally denied; he was polite to the end. It was there, however, and he expressed it not by an uncontrolled outburst but by leaving — and by his departure showed that he had no time for me.

I could only accept it and try to show him that he was controlling his negative feelings towards me as he did towards all women and explain my reasons for this conclusion. The parallel was in letting go sexually. I made it clear that I was willing to see him again if he wished, and that he had not destroyed me in the course of therapy.

Men's diffi- culties with climax Some answers emerged in a formal study by 19 of the Institute's most experienced women doctors who met with Tom Main regularly for two years to try to understand and develop a method for treating men with difficulties in achieving climax.

In a study of 22 men unable to ejaculate in the vagina [7], two main groups of problems emerged: those where treatment was wanted to increase their own sexual pleasure, and those whose wives wanted them to produce sperm in order to have a baby. We found these men had a high incidence of twinning and sibling rivalry; childhood resentments at the mother's inability to give the patient full attention because of the rival; and early lack of support from the father. There was also a history of a relationship with the woman doctor which appeared to reflect the need of such a patient to stimulate and promise much, yet ultimately to disappoint women.

Non-ejaculation was defined as inability to ejaculate in the vagina. Some patients could ejaculate with masturbation but not in the vagina. With others, masturbation in various ways led to ejaculation. Some ejaculated only with oral stimulation; some did not ejaculate at all and never had nocturnal emissions.

Twelve men who actively sought help for themselves had gone to considerable lengths to find it, consulting general practitioners, psychiatrists, urogenital departments, ministers and counselling services, before meeting our doctors. They wanted sexual pleasure and orgasmic release for themselves. All became able to ejaculate at will in the vagina after between one and six sessions. The ten who were pushed into coming by their wives were not helped by our treatment. A typical phrase was 'I cannot satisfy my wife.' Their wish was to please or placate the wife rather than to seek personal pleasure in sexual fulfilment. The wives did most of the talking and demanded that their husbands be made to ejaculate. The concern of all these patients was fertility, not pleasure. None improved.

The men could maintain an erection in prolonged and active intercourse, although some tended to become bored eventually. They were proud of this ability, but had little appreciation of the vagina or of shared feelings. The wives were sexually responsive and most had enjoyed multiple orgasms early in their marriages; but eventually they began to feel that something was not right. One wife said, 'He doesn't seem to be making love to me, he does it as a duty, it's a bit of a chore.' In general, the wives began to want their husbands to find pleasure in *them* — and they desired sperm both for their personal pleasure in it and for the chance it gave them to conceive. A number were interested in artifical insemination or had tried it. The unconscious hostility behind the non-ejaculation of these innocent, dutiful, thwarting husbands became apparent to the doctors only slowly.

Some feelings of distaste for fatherhood were openly declared in a few cases. These aroused the interest of the doctors and made them sensitive to more subtle clues. Sometimes this distaste was linked with ideas of their own fathers, as shadowy or inadequate figures who had walked out on mother or had died, leaving them unsupported by masculine role models to advance their own roles from mother's son to father. Despite a conventional and appropriate declared wish for a child, the problem had sometimes come into the open only when the wife had stopped the pill, or it only occurred at the fertile time of the month.

The patients' mothers were seen in general as being unappreciative of the son's wish to be valued by her, not attentive enough of his commitment to her, but requiring him to adapt to her wishes and orders, a mother to be placated by a resentfully obedient son.

In the doctor–patient relationship the man was invariably agreeable, obedient and apparently collaborative in the interview with the doctor, and raised her highest hopes that she could help him. She felt powerful and valued and was satisfied at the progress of her patient for several interviews. Then, slowly, she became frustrated at her inability to proceed further. Trained to be perceptive about her own role, she then noticed that she had sometimes been turned by his projections into an omniscient, demanding woman, her early optimism having been engendered by a man whose potency lay in making the woman want him and then by witholding himself from her.

Unable to please mother enough An unexpected finding was that of the 22 men, seven were born as a twin. The incidence of twinning in Britain is one in 80 births (1.25%), and the figure of 32% is significantly high. Many of the others had brothers and sisters of whom they had been jealous. In order to gain maternal approval when young, they had hidden their resentment at mother's neglect, had sought to be good appeasing children, yet had never felt they could please their mothers enough because of the rival. These men were unsure that what they had to offer was of value and they did not value or enjoy being themselves. Others had striven to prove themselves 'better' than their siblings. A few openly declared their fear of fatherhood and their rivalry with any baby to come. Their need to be the woman's one and only was sometimes astonishingly clear. In other cases they seemed perversely to resist this. One man bluntly put it: 'I don't want to share my wife with anyone else.' Another only resented the easily interpretable thought that his train-set in the spare bedroom would be removed if a baby came.

Masters and Johnson reported five of their 17 clients to be anxious products of people with severe religious scruples, although they did not state what they saw as the norm. Four of the 22 men in our study were keen church workers; others were interested in good, clean healthy sports like football, or solitary pastimes, which took them out at night, such as coarse fishing. These sports were enjoyed more than time with their wives.

Women doctors are accustomed to examining men's genitals without embarrassment when his complaint is a physical one such as a hernia. But with this sexual complaint, some doctors found themselves feeling ill at ease about it. We came to recognize that it was the patient's fear that the examination would be a sexual event which led to our unease, and we could then observe how some patients took off some of their defences as they removed their clothes and could express simple fears; 'I think I am rather small', or 'It looks smaller today.' One patient revealed that he could not look at his genitals in a mirror and that his downward view troubled him; one almost fainted with anxiety about retraction of the foreskin when the doctor put out her hand to examine his penis; another revealed his castration fear of damage to the glans, especially if rammed into a vaginal spasm.

Two of these men had experienced distressing enuresis and two others were unable to urinate in public toilets alongside others. A few had enjoyable urination and height fantasies. One, high up, urinated on those below; another climbed a ladder to fetch shoes from a shelf, but looked down at a naked older woman. He fell on her and had exciting intercourse (but did not ejaculate). Another related that he could ejaculate only when travelling on top of a bus. All these could be linked with the infantile rivalry and the need to be above and in a superior position to others.

Interestingly, the 12 men who were 'cured' gave the woman doctor little or no credit for the improvement. One reported he was cured only because his wife had 'closed her legs', another because she 'was not as wet as usual'. A third said he had cured himself with a book which described movement during intercourse, and a fourth put it down to the fact that he had stopped masturbating. The doctors, of course, became wiser as the study proceeded and increasingly came to see that their early optimism was diagnostic of the patient's psychological stimulation of women, and the later experience of being ignored as diagnostic of the patient's new sense of owing his prowess to nobody but himself, which was the objective. An important element in the therapy appeared to be the ability of the woman doctor to respect, listen to and understand what the man had to offer; to resist the collusive temptation to be eager and confident and to instruct him, but to interpret events in the doctor–patient relationship as these appeared. She also had to be able to accept the man's need to achieve and own potency rewards for himself, and to tolerate, as a mother with a son, his pride in his own achievements and his lack of appreciation of her help. She had to act as a humble co-worker with the patient, not as an all-knowing doctor whose reward was an obedient, grateful patient.

Following this study, those of us who train other doctors throughout the British Isles have recognized that non-ejaculation is very common, both in subfertility clinics and in special clinics for psychosexual problems. It is puzzling to contrast this with the experience of the American authorities, Masters and Johnson, who reported only 17 cases in 11 years. Perhaps this discrepancy is related to the degree of motivation required to attend. A light observation about the difficulties of such men was that 'men who don't come in bed don't come for help either'. Certainly, many like those quoted found it hard to seek help for themselves, and others either 'came' or admitted difficulty in 'coming' only when pressed by their partners.

Absent patient cured One fascinating case study from a colleague from Scotland began to throw further light on the role of the partners of men. She had not been a member of the study group, so her fresh approach to the couple, Jock and Jean, was not prejudiced by our discoveries. The American therapists' findings were already published, though, and when by the end of the first session she felt completely at sea, she arranged for a male co-therapist to work with her and embarked upon their regimen, recommending how the couple might manage intercourse — giving the woman responsibility for 'helping' her man to climax by active muscle movements, and so on. They had one session as a foursome after which Jock, a soldier, returned to his posting overseas and was not seen again. Since he had little choice in the matter it may not be fair to suggest that he, like Bill, voted with his feet; but the fact remained that despite the doctor's best efforts, the person who was apparently the patient had got away. She was left with the anger and misery of Jean, wanting her baby, her husband out of reach for a further long period.

At an impasse with Jock and Jean, the doctor had found herself turning to alternative solutions, which were of very little use to her or her patients. She reported her work of their two consultations to the seminar where we studied the unique events and feelings of the moment when Jock and Jean first sat with a woman doctor, and later with a woman doctor and the reinforcement she had sent for in her hour of need, the male clinical psychologist!

Returning to the drawing-board in this way, this highly skilled doctor realized as soon as she began to describe Jean and Jock that the diagnosis had in a sense been clear from the moment they walked in the first time. A referring doctor's letter had read: '*She* wants a baby and *he* can no longer produce an ejaculation (my italics) — and as Jean had bounced in, the husky Jock had followed tight-lipped, dragging his heels. It had been Jean who did all the talking and although she was apparently expressing her patience and sympathy with 'the puir laddie — he tries so hard', the doctor realized by the end of her report that in fact she had not heard a good word about him in Jean's account of 'his problem'. Jean had been unaware of how savage her criticisms of Jock must have seemed to him; contemptuous, almost, of his best efforts.

Group discussion showed my colleague how useless Jean had made her feel, too, and that it was in self-defence against this feeling that she had decided to bring in another therapist, a man, to help. My colleague recognized the demoralizing effect that Jean, in her frustration, was having on Jock. No wonder, she reflected, he felt more comfortable at a safe distance commanding his platoon. The doctor recalled that at their second visit, the one designed to make Jean 'more active and helpful', Jock had attended in uniform, stripes and all. 'Looking back', said the doctor, 'I thought it was brave of him to come not actually armed!' In the event, of course, the joint efforts of no less than three people to sort him out were doomed, for Jock, having attended obediently but said little, quit treatment. But Jean and her rage and disappointment, her sense of resentment towards this 'puir wee' six-foot husband, remained. The doctor was left with the originally complaining 'patient', and could only sit with her and listen to her and allow her to express her pain.

Gradually, she was able to show Jean that her attacks on Jock were not helping her to achieve her wishes. Somewhere along the way working with Jean alone was useful, for on one of Jock's weekend leaves, pregnancy was achieved, and 'Jean found herself interested in enjoying intercourse with him whether they conceived a baby or not. What impressed her colleagues was that this doctor had 'cured' a man's failure to ejaculate *in absentia* by helping his wife to relieve the pressure. The earlier attempt at treatment by reinforcing Jean's activity, which had clearly looked to Jock like 'dominance', had been far less effective.

Andy Warhol said, 'I always run into strong women who are looking for a weak man to dominate them.' Sadly, it seems that we do quite often too; and it is not amusing for them or their partners.

7

Mutual projections and defences against anxiety

Conflicting passions
Conditional arousal
Childhood confusions
Passive aggression

For Fiona and Franco it was fireworks all the way — for them in their marriage and for me working with them. I felt from the first moment I met them that they belonged in an American novel or film saga. They and their story seemed larger than life and working with them often left me shaking. They were in their thirties — rich, beautiful people, of the good Roman Catholic stock of immigrants to a new continent. Franco's family had originated generations before in Italy, Fiona's in Ireland. I have deliberately named him thus in order to invite in you fantasies of Godfathers, because, as I got to know these two better, I came to feel that they belonged in that kind of dark and violent world. I felt as if I had been sucked into a soap opera and could not switch off.

Fiona and Franco: conflict-ing passions

When we first met, these charming people were at great pains to show me how they loved each other and their children. Fiona explained at length, as Jean had explained in a different way, how patiently she had tried to bear with Franco in his impotence, and how deep had been her disappointment in their sexual life. With a religious family morality such as hers, she would not have dreamed of drifting into the extra marital affair that had so wounded Franco's pride had she not been desperate . . . Franco agreed, and his dark eyes clouded as he humbly admitted his increasing failure. He had tried everything, he said: pills, hypnotists, cold showers! I felt that at any moment he would literally beat his breast: 'Mea maxima culpa'. 'Of course', he said, 'I worshipped this woman from the start. I was

never very confident with girls, and looking back perhaps
it would have helped if we had not both been virgins when
we married. If only she could have been more help to me
. . . You see doctor, she has never given me any encouragement, never said she enjoyed it — I always felt like a rapist
with her. But since the children were born I thought we were
doing a bit better,' — almost whining now — 'and then this
other man coming along, well, I tell you frankly doctor, it
knocked the bottom out of my world.' Fiona's eyes flashed:
'Oh no, darling, I really can't say you were ever any better
. . . It was just that I found out with him what it could really
be like.' Instantly Franco, who you might think had begun
to show some spark of life in his mild criticism of Fiona's
early difficulties, withdrew into apology.

That was our first meeting, the friendly one! I tried to
show Fiona how contemptuously she put Franco down
despite her protestations of love. I tried too to show Franco
how interestingly he dealt with her, that clearly he had some
discontent of his own and that he might reasonably feel
entitled to give voice to some complaint. Yet he behaved
in this humble placating way with her and with me, and
at the first sign of her challenging his critical remarks had
collapsed into apology. They were surprised. Both saw only
the outer veneers in each other and were blind to the feelings
beneath. For a time communciations were reopened, but
Franco could still not 'perform' when Fiona was welcoming
— feeling, as he said, fear that he would fail to please her
yet again and comparing himself inevitably with the shadow
of her lover. But on closer questioning, it was not so
one-sided. He had had, once since their last visit, a really
good erection and had managed intercourse with vigour.
But Fiona had been unable to respond. It was rape, she said,
he wasn't making love to her, just using her.

As we talked, the fragile surface with which each struggled to be kindly — polite even — cracked, and the hatred
which had grown out of their mutual disappointment boiled
over in torrents of self-justification, rage and cruel abuse.

Condi- I could continue with a long, sad, painful story, which had
tional no hope of resolution at the time of writing. Suffice to say
arousal that Fiona had her own difficulties with sexual response
except in certain circumstances. The excitement of her illicit
relationship, so different from marriage and motherhood

and her respectable view of 'dutiful' sex, was easy for her. Sex for pleasure with a man who was associated in her mind with the 'good Catholic girl' aspect of her personality was doomed. She could not allow herself to feel aroused in that frame of mind. Franco, on the other hand, felt himself a 'poor little mother's boy' when confronted with a dissatisfied woman whom he might fail to placate. This was in fact one of the phrases which Fiona used to beat him with, as in her suffering she wielded her contempt like a club. But what a curious kind of 'poor little mother's boy', apparently 'obedient' in his brave efforts to slave at Fiona's feet but in fact 'downing tools' in passive aggression, defeating her hopes just as he defeated, cringingly but effectively, any attempt of mine to help or encourage him.

For Fiona too, my attempts to get in touch with her gentler fears, of trusting her deepest feelings to someone whom she felt was not 'strong' enough to cope, met with scorn and resistance, as though any woman who could see loving in such dependent terms was worthy only of ridicule and contempt. Sadly, with Franco and Fiona, we see an example of what may be called 'mutual projection'. People who have primary difficulties with their own feelings often seem to find each other, and having found each other, continue further to reinforce each other's problems. All the vulnerability, the 'weakness' in each of them, was seen by them as living, as it were, in Franco, despite his business success and physical strength. Both felt intolerant of dependence and neediness; Fiona feared her own deeply. Both agreed that it belonged in Franco, yet both despised it there. Conversely Franco, ill at ease with his own confident aggression towards demanding women, denied it to himself, felt it and indeed provoked it in Fiona, who was fertile ground; and both of them hated and feared it there. Shall we agree with their assessment that Fiona found herself a 'mother figure' to Franco, he a 'poor little mother's boy' to her? Certainly they were acting those roles together by the time I met them. But what kind of 'mother'; what kind of 'son'? This was a mother–son relationship bereft of tenderness or understanding. Franco's early history offered some reasons why he should see 'mothers' in this way. That was a long time ago, however, as it was a long time ago that Fiona learned to hate 'little mother's boys'.

Fiona's view was that, for as long as she had known his family, Franco's mother had 'spoiled him rotten'. No-one would have been good enough, she felt, for any of her sons. It might be said, of course, that no woman is ever good enough for any mother's son, nor a man for any father's daughter, but some manage equably. Franco denied any negative feelings or experiences in relation to his mother, though agreeing with Fiona that perhaps her overwhelming fussing and cooking for all her sons was perhaps a bit 'over the top'. As far back as he could remember, he had needed and been given her approval. His father he remembered as a warm, rowdy, jolly man. That he was away during the week and had to deliver the beltings for the sons' sins of the week on his return seemed to Franco 'only natural'. He reported no sense of betrayal by his idealized mother about this. His one recollection as to why he was 'belted' was for hitting one of his new baby sisters in her pram when he was about four years old.

We may assume that Franco's pattern of dealing with the trials and value systems of life had been established to some degree by then. At what age — or rather at what stage of emotional development — can we expect consciously to comprehend our reactions and make sense of them? Most of the people I have described so far ran into some doubts about themselves in adolescence — the stage at which the desires and the physical awareness of adult sexuality are beginning to stir. None of them had any serious doubts that they were loved and valued, whatever their shortcomings, before that. Thus they learned, even if not fully consciously, what seemed the 'good' and acceptable and the 'bad' and unacceptable aspects of their personalities at a stage of their development when some conscious and practical reasoning could apply. Belinda (Chapter 5), for example, had reason to fear what becoming a woman might entail, but never that as long as she did her best she would fail to be appreciated. In contrast James (Chapter 3), who felt 'sent away' to school at seven, was aware that much of his uncertainty at that age was about not understanding why this 'rejection', as he felt it, had been necessary. It was to be 'good for him', he was told, and he must be 'brave'. Another man I knew with a very similar story to James's had been put on the train to his first prep school at the age of seven, dressed in his new and strange uniform, and told, as his weeping mother kissed him goodbye, that his elder brother was taking him to a party. These conflicting messages might have been less confusing had they thought to tell his brother of the lie.

The brother, himself only nine, was unprepared and unable to help when school fellows on the train howled with derisive laughter at the youngster's innocent question as to where the party was to be.

I draw attention to the idea that, when things go wrong for children, it is incomprehension which may be the worst torment. In this lost situation, children tend in their puzzling to feel whatever has gone wrong must be their fault, as parents are seen up to a certain age as all-powerful. Child psychiatrists could make a more informed guess than I can as to when these troubles arise in individual children. It varies from child to child, but that there will be for each one an age below which comprehension is impossible. As the child's attempts at reasoning fail, the experience, the feeling — which is the only reality — takes on a nightmare quality, and they can only deal with it as they may. We all have less drastic recollections of trying to deal with such confusions as a child. We walk on the lines of the pavements or avoid walking on them. We make bets and promises and bargains with ourselves or God, feeling that if *we* can get things right, the rest will fall into place. Those parts of us that we suspect as causative of trouble will vary, but will often seem related to our rebellious, angry, even murderous feelings towards those of our loved ones who have betrayed us. *Childhood confusions*

What can a seven-year-old or a four-year-old know of rage and murder? Well, Franco had not apparently entirely lost touch with his capacity for rage at four, since he did get round to hitting the interloping sister! One can only speculate about the effect if his mother had given him a sharp slap in righteous wrath at the time, and subsequently loved and forgiven him. Perhaps it would have been clearer to him had he understood the nature of his crime. It was natural enough to be fed up with his rival, but, despite his naughtiness, such dreadful feelings did not cast him altogether out of love. It seems however that he picked up the message that angry, destructive and envious feelings were bad, not only from the cold-blooded delayed punishments from father, but from the coldness and control of his mother's immediate response. Further, that the father he loved and longed to see greeted him with the strap cannot have helped him feel easy about male aggression. Yet rage and envy are a normal part of human response:

no-one who has seen a frustrated new-born baby scream for the breast can seriously label it fear or even hurt alone. Red in the face, fists and feet flailing — is this vulnerable frailty or the epitome of uncontrolled fury? It is a saintly mother who has never known, and been terrified by, her own awareness that at two o'clock in the morning, she is tempted to hit back.

Knowledge of what babies can feel is developing rapidly. R.D. Laing is held to believe that emotional disturbance can be traced back before birth, even to the blastocyst. Leboyere's stated views on the best ambience for the new-born child are based on similar ideas — that the child can be welcomed from the silence of the womb with soft lights and sweet music to lessen the shock of being cast rudely out, although Tom Main wryly points out that the uterus is more likely to be a deafeningly noisy environment, with the lub-dups of the mother's heart beat, the surging of torrents in the placental blood vessels, and the gurgling of bowels. Either way, why should they not, above and beyond the need to gasp for air and inflate their lungs, scream with fury at being squashed through a tunnel, possibly with injury, and cast out into a foreign environment which, however we construct it, will be unfamiliar?

Control of infantile wishes and passions does, of course, have to be learned, and our response to them forms much of the burden of upbringing. We cannot continue indefinitely to scream for the breast whenever we feel the need for comfort or nourishment and expect to get it. We may neither excrete upon the floor where we stand, nor kick and hit and bite in frustration. If we learn these things, knowing inside ourselves that we are safe, loved and valued even as we fail, we can learn to use that control, that frustration, not only to behave in an increasingly adult and 'civilized' way, but creatively, as a fund of energy and tension which we can draw on to express other growth needs and activities. But, if in learning we feel that our failures to conform cast us truly out of love; that there is no comprehensible explanation, no consistency, no kiss and make up, or that a younger intruder now seems adored for those very activities for which we are now punished, we should not be surprised if development of such comfortable inner controls comes to grief. Anything which resonates with the need for such control or the fear of its loss continues to give us unconscious confusion and leads us to inappropriate, even childlike responses in later life.

Had Franco been prepared to seek full psychoanalysis, I might have some concrete evidence as to the relevance of these theoretical speculations to the man he had become. For me, the only hard facts were that the man before me dealt with women he 'could not please' — with Fiona and with me — in a characteristic way. We saw nothing of the confident fist-flailing by now. With his back to the wall, as it felt to him, Franco responded by crawling and placating, 'humbly', like Uriah Heep. His hatred was felt by me, and he was freed a little, temporarily, by my observation of it not as a criticism but as an interesting clinical fact about him. For a week he could see the livelier potential of his aggression, and his penis responded — once!

This 'downing tools' reaction is another facet of male *Passive* impotence which I often come across. It is very different, *aggres-* I believe, from the fearful and anxious reaction of other men. *sion* I have also referred to it as the Gandhi syndrome, and mean that as a compliment! Trade Unionists, frustrated by their 'masters' and with no other weapon at their disposal than the withdrawal of their labour, go on strike by 'downing tools'. That to withdraw labour and literally down tools can be read equally in basic sexual language is evident; less so is the unconscious process which can literally lead to the downing of the sexual tool in a passively aggressive, unconsciously stubborn way. Nevertheless it is an idea that I have often shared fruitfully with men who complain of impotence when under pressure. More often still, for they are under pressure then by definition, I have found myself sharing it with men whose wives, like Fiona, are complaining of their impotence. How can I make such a diagnosis with confidence — for if the observation is inaccurate for an individual man, it will of course be as useless as the wrong antibiotic for a specific infection? The key is by observation of how the man deals with me in the here and now of the interview. Some men, for example, might feel confident to quiz me about my qualifications, might reasonably feel entitled to know what kind of therapist I am. Some might, if our first consultation was not to their satisfaction, return and report honestly to me that it was a waste of time. Others, like Bill and Jock (Chapter 6), who could not be quite so straightforward, might decide with their feet. Franco stayed in obedience, as he would see it, to Fiona's and my wishes; but how powerfully he defeated our efforts with his submissive manner. How much more easily could I or Fiona have challenged him if he had retaliated. This is the situation that reminds me of the great Mahatma Gandhi, the father of non-violent protest, who began the overthrow of one of the world's greatest empires, when force of arms had failed, by sitting in the street. Can we call this 'weakness'? If so, far from despising it we may pray to be saved from those we call 'stronger'!

Enraged Having acknowledged that I was briefly of help to Franco,
by since he left our first meeting and had his first good erection
blandness in years, but recognizing too that his symptomatic improvement changed the relationship for the better not at all, we
must look back again to Fiona and ask ourselves what she
was up to in rejecting him at the moment he delivered the
goods she had so vociferously ordered. We can identify with
her a bit, for I too could have been easily enraged by Franco's
blandness, and had indeed pointed out to him how busy
and bossy he seemed to invite me to be, only then to defeat
me with his sweet-faced apologies. Such confrontation can
rebound on the 'accuser' making both therapist and wife
feel unjustifiably 'bitchy'. But Fiona, without the benefit of
the years of training despite which even I was in danger of
reacting to Franco, had her own style of reaction. Seeing
the 'poor little mother's boy' in action, she was not merely
irritated but provoked to frenzy and contempt; and in the
doing, of course, multiplied and perpetuated the reaction
she so disliked, thus being provoked even further. Again
there were hints that Fiona had her own early reasons for
this. Her difficulty in acknowledging calmly and consciously
her need for a different kind of man and her contempt for
her own 'weakness' were clear to me. Alas, the temperature
of this barely concealed marital warfare was such that my
attempts to get in touch with her pain were also doomed.
Her fear that to show needs and tenderness was dangerous
and would lead to submission and defeat was deep enough
in herself. With Franco, who actually did fail to respond,
her difficulties were compounded.

Fiona, it emerged, was the fourth of a line of regularly
spaced daughters. The baby of these, and the pretty one,
it seemed likely that for the early years of her life she was
much fussed and adored, whatever her tantrums, by both

parents and older sisters, not only for her charms but for being the family baby. Her mother had then had a miscarriage, and when Fiona was three and a half, their first son had been born.

I have no direct evidence as to the effect of this upon Fiona's development. However I have met so many others with comparable histories that I can speculate with some confidence that at that early age it would be reasonable to suppose that 'her nose was put out of joint', she felt displaced. So many girls grow up with the feeling that the much-wanted son was the important one and that on his arrival the sense of being the family star was suddenly withdrawn. When a feeling that to be a boy is better is experienced, what might have been easy, uninhibited sibling rivalry is self-perpetuating through lack of rational understanding, colouring a girl's whole vision of the value of the sexes and causing her to look on her own sexuality as second-class.

In our first study we came to believe that patients such as these threw new light on the concept Freud described as 'penis envy'. Freud had noticed, among his patients, women who revealed the need to denigrate and challenge not only the penis itself in an inability to welcome and enjoy it sexually, but also in terms of what it represented of men's perceived advantages over women. We met many such women too, and our experience of them confirmed Freud's view that certain qualities — hardness, assertive drive, competitiveness, intellect and rationality — were seen as 'masculine', and if not as admirable, certainly as enviable and to be feared and resisted.

We found, however, more than a sense of second-class citizenship in women who felt this way. We made interpretations of their need to envy, to challenge and to resent these 'masculine' qualities. We found then that such women often revealed deeper anxieties about valuing and trusting other qualities which they saw as 'feminine' and thus vulnerable, worthy of contempt. Such qualities were softness, 'wetness', receptivity, emotional feeling and responsiveness, soppiness, tenderness. If such women could be helped to find the courage to face and enjoy these parts of themselves, their need to control and challenge their men was relieved. This idea is explored again in Chapter 10.

We came to see Freud's view not as a fundamental and unchangeable fact of sexual life but frequently as a defensive system against the greater difficulty in realizing the enjoyment of being a woman. Even today it is common to label these aspects of human nature as 'masculine'and 'feminine' and to enjoy or resist and fear them in the opposite sex according to our own individual confidence in being who we are. R.D. Laing's film *Birth*, for example, implies that if all births were managed by women, loving kindness would prevail. As I have stressed, it is not my experience that women have a monopoly on tenderness or gentleness any more than men have a monopoly on assertiveness or exploitative competition. People vary. And today we recognize the other side of the coin of sexual envy. Many men admit to feeling deep envy for women's capacity to carry and give birth to children, causing them defensively to challenge and derogate in their turn.

None of us can ever hope to know exactly how it feels to be the other sex. We can only imagine, and — if sharing in love or in childbirth is emotionally close enough — sense dimly the deepest feelings of the other. If we are lucky enough to feel total contentment in our own sexuality, we may then begin to enjoy rather than to envy or despise these complementary qualities in our partners.

Nor do these early pains of sibling rivalry confine themselves to the battle of the sexes. Fiona was the youngest — the baby, the star — for just three years and a bit. What eldest child is ever the baby, the main recipient of attention, for long enough, whatever the actual age gap before the arrival of the interloper? What is enough? One year? At least at one year mother cannot avoid sharing some picking up and cuddling, some help with feeling. Five years? So that the newcomer's claims for personal cosseting, until now our sole prerogative, coincide with the rough, worrying world of starting school? What of twins, who never have sole attention? It sounds as though at least some of our nonejaculators found it difficult. I touch on this here because as with Fiona and Franco, such events have their effect on the people we become as adults, upon the inner strengths and weaknesses and the styles with which we deal with our developing sexuality. Difficulties at this depth will also tend to make people less able to respond to the more straightforward interpretations of brief psychosexual treatment.

When I say brief psychosexual treatment, I do mean brief, *Entren-*
not only in relation to classic psychoanalysis or *ched*
psychotherapy, but to behavioural programmes also. I refer *defences*
to from three to six sessions, or 12 at the most. As seen from *against*
earlier cases, one may suffice. Michael Balint suggested we *vulnera-*
consider in diagnosis and prognosis, 'Take away the sexual *bility*
problem and what have you got?' We may agree that for
Franco and Fiona there are many problems meriting attention. I have suggested that both these two had long-standing
reasons for their obedience to and unconscious hatred of
parental values; both were entrenched in their defences
against vulnerability. Both needed some patient and detailed
examination of why they had become the people they had
become. Their difficulties in the confident enjoyment of
adult sexuality were only symptoms of this, the merest tip
of an iceberg. Further, their sexual difficulties as a pair were
merely the overt expression of their difficulties in relating
in other ways. Their marital warfare was intense indeed,
and their individual and compounded need to avoid facing
this, to keep a collusive belief in love and duty and
sweetness, was deeply painful and mutually destructive.

Group marital therapy was arranged for them, but sadly
the pattern was repeated and reinforced there too. Eventually they parted. Predictably, perhaps, it was Fiona, now
easier with her rage and disappointment, who gave up and
started a new life with the children and a man who could
be less terrorized by her clamour. This I guess was due partly
to the male half of the marital therapy team, who fought
her head on without being destroyed by her constant
challenges, and partly by his wife and co-therapist, a gentle,
clever woman who may have shown Fiona that it is possible
to reveal vulnerability without becoming either a door-mat
or a mere handmaiden to a man of power. Unfortunately
Franco could not take such confrontation: usually 'too busy'
to attend sessions, he sulked and invited sympathy when
he did. After Fiona quit, he went home to mother, literally,
for a while, metaphorically, altogether. When I last heard,
he had clearly found there the sympathy he needed and the
warfare continued in a kind of sad, long-distance wrangling
over money and children, his family still spreading the word
on his behalf about how badly this scarlet woman had
treated him.

Let us abandon Franco and Fiona; I can bear them no
longer. They are too painful and cruel and I was such a

failure to them . . . Yet in all honesty I cannot do so without observing and considering my last remarks on Franco — how cruel and contemptuous I have deliberately worded them. This is the effect he had on people around him, *in his pain*. How difficult it is, even with training, to remember the tragedy; the sadness and loneliness and the desire within people with unattractive defences to be different. Fiona, in *her* pain, was unquestionably savage, cruel and contemptuous. She, you will recall, had the same shattering effect on me as she did on Franco, despite my attempts to help, to understand, with the skills at my disposal. It is well to remember that although therapists cannot hope to 'cure' everyone, although friends or relations cannot hope to help or understand or even like everyone, that people are not, on the whole, hateful on purpose. And for ourselves, 'mutual projection' is a simple fact of everyday life that we may sometimes come to comprehend in our own lives.

8

The excitement and terror of violence

The temptation to batter children
Religious beliefs blamed
Sado-masochism
Perversions or preferences?

It is a fair working rule that in so far as we feel uneasy about *Projected* an inner aspect of our own personality, we feel at least *feelings* equally uneasy when we recognize it in others. It was, in effect, easier for Fiona to see 'weaknesses' and despise them 'out there' in another, than to face the pain of acknowledging them within herself. Many others like her, were they easier with their own feelings of uncertainty, could allow their partners their strengths, could allow themselves to be 'taken care of' in therapy as in bed, and to feel good in that situation.

Conversely Franco and others like him, so fearful of or unaware of their negative aggressive feelings, hating them in themselves, find it easier to hate them in others, and to see them as Franco saw them in Fiona, even provoked them in Fiona, and feared and fought them there as his own projections. The alternative would have been a painful awareness that the fight, the fear and the hatred, was with those frightening aspects of himself.

Throughout our studies we have often wondered whether these factors — intolerance of one's own inner 'babyishness' leading to fear and hatred when recognized in actual babies — could have any relevance to baby-battering. I have no researched evidence, for people who actually batter their babies rarely find their ways to doctors like us, nor am I suggesting that they should. I have however met many women and men for whom their *fear* of battering babies, or indeed their husbands or wives, is a vivid and potent aspect of the anxieties they express. For such people, it is my experience that they see, in their babies or partners, some aspects of themselves of which they are deeply and unconsciously intolerant. Panicking at the strength of their emotions, they fear that they really will express themselves violently, even while realistically aware that the potential victim is not doing anything very dreadful.

Two women are good examples. One I knew very little. She was lovely, talented and intelligent, and had no sexual difficulty whatever. Her relationship with her husband and sons was fine. Since her daughter's birth however she had found affection towards this child impossible, had felt tempted to push her away even from the moment she first put her to the breast. That she was a particularly cuddly, dribbly, tactile child made the relationship all the more difficult, since the mother's coolness only further agitated the childs's need for physical warmth and reassurance. Inevitably, by the time the daughter's sexuality began to emerge, with masturbation and normal childish curiosity, her mother found her good intentions to be accepting impossible. It was clear that for whatever reason this very competent and controlled woman had felt intolerant of the clinging aspects of her own femininity to the point where seeing them in her daughter caused active revulsion.

The temp- The other I knew much better. Courageously, over many
tation to years she had sought analytic help. Hers was a long and
batter subtle story, a triumph for her persistence in becoming her
children own woman and competent as a mother, despite a background which had come close to destroying other members of the family mentally. She had sought analysis originally when she became aware of her temptation to batter her children. Physically, she resisted this compulsion; mentally she recognized that she might harm them equally by her confused emotions. Her sexual life was never a problem: always loving and orgasmic, it represented safe ground, in contrast to others I have described for whom that kind of abandonment and sense of acceptance was in itself a difficulty.

To cut a long and complex story very short, her identification with the violence she felt in her father, who loved her turbulently, and who had himself died violently, had highly complex implications for her. On the one hand, her excitement in it, her vision of it as a mother mixed-up with his expressions of love and attention in contrast to a mother, cool, controlled and, to her as a child, apparently unconcerned, caused great difficulty for her when confronted with the need to care for children of her own. Yet along with her excitement in violence there was, of course, terror and child-like incomprehension, not only of the violence itself but of her own attraction to it. This conflicted with a wish to be appreciated by her mother, a goal she felt she could only achieve if she was controlled, ladylike and 'better'. By the time I met her, she was well aware, thanks to her analysts, of how the disorganized behaviour which her children, like all children, showed threw her into a nightmare confusion of reaction, not least because of her own need to be responsible for them.

In touching on the impact on children of outside, ill-understood events that are perceived by them to be their fault, a frequent factor seems to be the child's feeling of responsibility for their parents' troubles before they are old enough to understand, at an age when they might still reasonably be able to trust their parents to take care of *them*. I repeat my own view that, generally speaking, parents vary and that none are perfect, so that a child's reactions will to some extent be related to that child's inner capacities. This is not the place to debate the whole nature versus nurture question, but it is true that given broadly the same set of parents and the same circumstances children develop differing ways of learning to cope. To take my last patient's family, she came through with determination and at great cost, while another member of the same family found his own path, it would seem, with some confidence, and another fell into severe mental illness. Every mother knows that she can advise two of her children to take raincoats on a day when storm clouds are gathering. One may rebelliously choose not to and be drenched, and another will swelter obediently in the heat, though the clouds pass over. *The child's sense of responsibility*

When Freddie and Frances, both nearing forty, first consulted my colleague, their marriage was polite — just. As with Franco and Fiona, intense warfare was not far from the surface, painfully concealed beneath a veneer by which two decent people tried in vain to salvage some hope of a future together. But theirs proved to be warfare of a very different kind, cold and intransigent on both sides. Neither *Freddie and Frances: warfare of a different kind* my colleague nor I was much help to them. Nor, when I last heard, was a highly skilled, analytically trained team of marital therapists. These were two responsible people who had once been fond of each other and who had kept trying when things began to go wrong. They had achieved a workable friendship. Both Freddie and Frances had deep-seated difficulties of their own with the capacity to relate warmly and confidently to one another. Their sexual problem was merely a symptom of other problems. On the surface their personalities seemed to be a good match. Alas, that their defensive systems played into each other's meant that as these veneers gradually slipped away, the underlying problems for each played into each other's also. Thus, as with Franco and Fiona, the difficulties of each reinforced those of the other: mutually provoking, mutually destroying.

Maybe Freddie and Frances would have survived better had they been left well alone. I stress this because there is a danger in a climate of high expectations, where a wide and sometimes wild variety of help is available, that there may be some pressures upon couples to look for more from their relationships than is possible. I must repeat once again that psychosexual doctors have no special magic or panacea on offer. We can help some people a bit, just as all professional workers hope to help some people a bit, and for some people, to be allowed to let off steam to anyone — to a friend or neighbour — may be enough. For Freddie and Frances, however, having to face their difficulties, to become aware that all their dreams were cold, was not an experience anyone should be invited to undertake lightly.

Mutual hatred They were not, of course, obliged to do so. They came to my colleague because they hoped for a baby, and neither was fully fertile. Frances did not ovulate regularly, a problem which might have been simply solved if all else were well. Freddie's sperm count was low, not helped by the fact that he was overweight and becoming more so as his social drinking increased. Again, were all else well, this might have been improved with simple physical measures, but the necessity for these investigations brought to light that they made love seldom. Frances had to insist on attempting intercourse at mid-month, a process that she found humiliating because her irregular ovulations were almost impossible to chart. Freddie's erections, less confident than ever, failed every time. Frances would weep, Freddie would pour himself another gin and tonic. Both tried to be patient and civilized, but resentment and guilt about that resentment, exacerbated by the need in both to control such untidy feelings for their own reasons, led to a chill withdrawal into what could only, however unconscious, be described as mutual hatred. It was awful for them; but the passive withdrawal of Freddie and the sanctimonious, tearful martyrdom of Frances — which was the way each felt and saw each other — was deeply destructive to any chance of returning to the amicable separate lives in harness by which their marriage had survived hitherto.

Freddie, who started life as a salesman, was now a successful entrepreneur in the rough world of advertising: he described himself as a 'media man'. He was a pillar of his golf club, an after-dinner speaker, full of bonhomie but, in Frances's view, 'never home when I want him'. In his early manhood he had had no trouble 'pulling the birds' (his phrase). He hinted at his prowess among the 'dollies' of the King's Road in the 'sixties', and later among the 'arties and intellectuals' (his words again) of Camden Town. But here was real life: a real woman who required more than the talents of the chase and the one-night-stand. I found it hard to believe that Freddie could have sold anything to me, for in the vulnerable situation of help-seeking and the humiliation of confessing his sexual failures, a very different man was revealed. Who can blame him? Here was not an eager volunteer, seeking personal help for his own greater enjoyment. Freddie was here placatingly, reluctantly, hoping to please and satisfy his wife's wishes; willing to do his best but with little personal enthusiasm either for sex with this woman or for fatherhood.

It is not surprising that in such a threatening interview with now two powerful women wanting, as he saw it, to bring him to heel, Freddie's well-tried social skills should appear merely sycophantic. But his fear of women, or the fear of his feelings towards them, which may be easily interpretable for some, was not so easy for Freddie, and the feeling which came across was one of deep entrenched dislike. Nor did it seem useful to attack him with such accusations, knowing

Fear of women

that I could not offer him the prolonged and detailed support of intensive psychoanalyis even should he wish it. As it turned out Frances did the attacking for both of us. Smiling sweetly, she called him 'an ageing trendy', and 'a sheep in wolves' clothing'. There was a terrible and cruel truth in these remarks.

I have alluded earlier (Chapter 3) to the idea, easy to comprehend for a trained therapist but often deeply threatening to others, that 'homosexuality' is merely a technical description of the element in all of us which prefers the company of and enjoys affection for members of our own sex. Conversely, as with the likes of Freddie, it may be reflected in terms of dislike (in unconscious depth) of the opposite sex. But for Freddie and his like, to explore this with sensitivity and skill would take time and care and patience. To drop the word in a single diagnostic interview might be quite devastating — too difficult for him even to hear, let alone understand. For Freddie was not 'homosexual' in the usual sense of the word. Indeed he was deeply critical of those he called with true abhorrence 'fairies'. He felt no sexual attraction to men whatever, being possibly too critical of any such feelings in himself, even in non-sexual terms, to face them at all. Further, much of his self-esteem as a man had rested upon his success with women earlier.

I was told years ago of an idealistic young man who had the accusation that he feared his own homosexuality tossed at him casually and with amusement by some 'amateur psychologist' at a pseudo-religious cult's encounter group. He paled briefly and later walked from the meeting to the station with apparent calm. There, I was told, he threw himself under a train. Whether true or apocryphal, this tragic tale is, I believe, a cautionary one. Quasi-religious, quasi-psychological cults and 'treatments' are springing up all over the world in seemingly epidemic numbers, and vulnerable people — particularly the young — are more likely than others to seek such magic remedies. It is essential that anyone who offers 'care' of a kind which may resonate unwittingly with the unconscious has appropriate training and is answerable to a professional body. If they are not prepared to do so, then they must be answerable to the law of the land. Nor would I exclude myself or any other medical graduate from that accountability.

Frances was, Freddie said, 'a virtuous woman'. No crime, one might think, but on his lips the remark was a scornful accusation. We have noticed by now that so many men, like Freddie and Franco and others, who apparently behave as sexual lions and are confident with girls who are 'easy' in their unquestioning admiration, actually need a great deal of encouragement and reassurance. Whatever Frances' high moral standards had brought to the marriage in terms of dedication and devotion, the sexual passivity which went with them had not provided that encouragement for Freddie. How difficult it was for her to see this. She saw Freddie as experienced, and sex itself as the man's responsibility. It was hard enough for her to understand that her 'virtue' came across to him as 'coldness'. Freddie's own difficulty in acknowledging even to himself that his success with casual flirtations was because they demanded less of him, made it even harder for him to see the fear and shyness, the sexual innocence and ignorance which lay behind Frances' 'wilful' prudishness.

It is a sad irony that it is these very outer traits which may have provided the initial mutual attraction. We may speculate that Frances may have hoped that an apparent sophisticate like Freddie would overcome her 'virtuous' inhibitions; that he might teach her and take care of her and eventually sweep her off her feet. And Freddie, with his own inner need to find a 'sweet little thing' who would look up to him and trust herself to him unquestioningly, might well have felt more confident with the virginal girlishness of Frances, with whom he could feel truly in charge.

Frances was a devout Christian of a somewhat funda- *Religious* mentalist, evangelical, puritanical bent. That she chose this *beliefs* path from within a family background of the Church of *blamed* England obviates the necessity for me to seem to criticize any one 'branch' or another, nor would I if I could. It is easy and tempting to blame a church, as it is easy and tempting to blame, say, parents, for the beliefs and consequent attitudes of their followers. Frances attributed her anti-sex feelings to her religious beliefs, quoting St Paul's saying that 'it is better to marry than to burn', as he indeed wrote to the believers in Corinth, the 'sin city' of the day! She did *not* quote Jesus' reference to the Old Testament encouragement: 'For this you leave your father and mother and become one flesh' (not, you will note, 'one pair of communicants' but 'one flesh'), nor the erotic poetry of the Song of Solomon. We hear, in religion too, what we wish to hear, and quote to support an argument reflecting our inner needs.

Frances had been a virgin into her thirties, and why should she not? Her enthusiasm for sex was modest: she saw it as a duty, and a nose-wrinkling one at that, permissible only for the procreation of children. She had never reached orgasm, even in their more active early days, and saw no need for it now. That her man's enjoyment might be greater if it gave her equal pleasure was a foreign idea to her, and in contrast to some who can review their attitudes to this in response to new insights, Frances did not want to know. I felt positively immoral in suggesting it — a projection coming very clearly from Frances' own value systems about her own potential sexuality, that this aspect of her was indeed whorish and she would have none of it. The sadness was that she took great delight in Freddie's climax in the days when he was able to have them. She felt, she said, that she had 'given' herself for him and had 'given' him such pleasure. She simply could not understand that this was not enough to make him feel rewarded.

The motto of my own medical school is *'Dare quam accipere'*: it is better to give than to receive. This is true in many facts of social life, but is flawed as a sexual imperative for those who are unclear as to what that 'gift' is, in this case, the giving of oneself wholly.

Frances' confusion about a woman's role as a sexual 'giver' is a common one. She could not distinguish between giving Freddie the use of her body for the pleasure of his orgasm on the one hand, and giving him the pleasure of pleasing her on the other. Yet we have all, I think, experienced the disappointment caused by a friend who always refuses a compliment or an offer of help. In their 'unselfishness', how spurned and useless they make us feel. Who would wittingly rob a child of those proud moments when their home-made Christmas present for us emerges from their gummy bundle?

Sado-
maso-
chism I have hinted that sado-masochism, like homosexuality, is an aspect of human personality and behaviour which quite commonly crops up, or stirs anxiously below the surface, in many a discussion of the sexual difficulties of otherwise

sane and healthy people. However, 'sado-masochist' too has crept into everyday language as a casual, pseudo-psychological label for individual human beings. As with other such labels — 'queer' or 'neurotic' — we may do well to stop and reflect that if, in our own prejudices, we imply value judgements, those judgements should at least be based upon accuracy.

I have met people for whom their backgrounds of culture or cult involved, for example, vengeance unto death upon the breaker of an arranged engagement, or personal scourging as a self-punishment for masturbation in adolescence, leading to horrifying scars which to the individual concerned were badges of manhood and pride. But it is rare to take pleasure in such savagery; more often the terror of it is only exceeded by the terror that it might become a source of pleasure. This can lead to a more general inhibition of any abandoned and uncontrolled sexual emotion which might lead to abandonment of controls on that much more prohibited pleasure in savagery and pain. Some people, like Belinda, come to accept violence as simply an unattractive fact of life. Probation officers and policemen meet many for whom the everyday language of communication is the drunken punch-up after the Friday night pay-packet. Rarely is this the outward expression of any true taste for the infliction or receiving of pain, be it physical or emotional. Nor if, as some hold, wife-battering is sometimes invited, physically or emotionally, is it often consciously so.

I meet many men who have felt that the fears and the confused excitement of corporal punishment may have given them some dire taste for perversion. Sometimes finding in their otherwise happy adult sexual lives a taste for playful spanking or being spanked, they label themselves 'sadists' or 'masochists' with shame and self-disgust. This shame and self-disgust may then pose a far greater problem for them than the fairly innocent sexual preference in itself.

We have seen that cold attempts to repress the resentment which can result from mutual disappointment can have a truly destructive effect on relationships. There is often less cruelty in a few fair physical fights, with the freedom to kiss and make up with pleasure and excitement, than in sitting upon violent feelings. The distinction needs to be made here between those who may find some fun in the sharing of any attitude we may label 'perversion', and those for whom the pleasure is in insisting on it despite the wishes of the other. The witholding of simple pleasure of any kind, however apparently justified by virtue, may be more sadistic in effect than in a lifetime of mutually enjoyed off-beat frolics. Furthermore, that coldness with which some take satisfaction in martyrdom — we cannot call it pleasure — may be more punitive, more destructive of a happy relationship, than any sense of erotic fun in being overpowered or bullied a bit. Remember the unconscious masochism with which Frances saw her role as a frigid but virtuous wife.

Perver- How can we define perversion? I hope I make it clear that
sions or I do not subscribe to the 'whatever turns you on' school of
prefer- thought. Truly sadistic practices can be dangerous. If an
ences individual's only path to orgasm is, for example, the savaging of a child, clearly society must have a judgemental view. But we may also note Tom Main's dictum, 'There is none so cruel as a frightened man'. An army psychiatrist in wartime, he pointed out that people may even kill if their terror is great enough. And who has not seen a mother who has nearly led her toddler into the path of oncoming traffic. How she beats the child, in her own panic!

Criminal psychopathology is not the concern of this book or of psychosexual medicine, but we do often meet disgust and self-disgust in people's attitudes to sex which are more difficult to ease than simple distaste. They may make intercourse an unattractive aim, even for some who intellectually wish to achieve it. I have met many women who reach orgasm easily by external stimulation of the clitoris but whose feeling about the vagina and its inner sensations is one of deep disgust rather than fear. Clearly guilt or shame from their early masturbatory experiences cannot be the simple answer, since it has not interfered with their continued enjoyment of these external pleasures, only with their deepest motivation for change. Likewise men whose imagining of the unknown, unseen and internal is tainted by true disgust may be poorly motivated for change, and unable to alter this view.

Keith, who became impotent after his wife's difficulties with vaginismus had been treated, saw the vagina as raw flesh — but more than that, his phantasy of intercourse was that he would be sucked in, held, trapped. He felt that he might be out of control forever: lost and unable to escape. His wife, in her own frightened spasm, had seemed to him safe, undemanding, even to be protected. But as soon as her vagina became accessible and she became eager, in Keith's view, his own problem was inescapably revealed.

Oral sex is another matter in which disgust may disturb otherwise carefree sexual lives. Many couples find great mutual pleasure in genital kissing in its own right and as part of mutual arousal. Many too find pleasure in reaching climax in this way. But if it is important to one and disgusting to the other, much distress and shameful secondary self-doubt can arise. I meet women for whom the idea of accepting an emission in their mouth is truly loathsome — and if this is something their men really enjoy, they have a problem. I have met some women for whom the intensity of their own disgust led them to try to understand it, irrespective of their wishes to please their men. Several had quite evident troubles with their relationships to their mothers as regards breast-feeding and had themselves some revulsion towards feeding their own babies. The nature of their phantasy communications evoked a fantasy in me that somehow their difficulties in sucking and swallowing this other 'milk' might have primitive roots in their infantile impressions of the breast. I offer this as an idea, not as a serious hypothesis. Perhaps an analyst of the future may find it worthy of study.

Furthermore, there are men who find themselves unable to respond to their women's taste for genital kissing. I have met men for whom the difficulty is intense enough for them to wonder at their revulsion by a part of a woman they otherwise adore. Not surprisingly, those who have less than fully conscious negative attitudes towards the nature of female sexual organs will have difficulty in coming so closely face-to-face with them. I have met, too, some for whom the association with excretory function makes the idea of such kissing not only unattractive but deeply abhorrent. Some such men and women have found oral sex easier to accept after looking at these awkward ideas calmly, perhaps even finding some humour in them. For others it has been important to understand why what for most would be an optional extra, is so vital for the partner who cannot manage without this very specific stimulation.

As with so many other aspects of sexual preference, those who are reasonably comfortable with their particular quirks and those of their partners will find their own compromises without the need for professional consultation — but to suggest that there are always easy solutions for some who experience unhappiness so deep as those I have described would be cruelty indeed.

Part Three

CASE PROFILES OF THE PITFALLS
IN ESTABLISHED RELATIONSHIPS

9

The loss of passion

Friendship remains
Loss of inner privacy
The intrusion of parental blessing
The fear of risking trust
Rivalling parents

I turn in this final section to the problems of those – young *To suffer* and old – whose sexual lives have been happily establish- *passively* ed, but have later gone wrong. For us all, life and circum- *or oppose* stances, both internal and external, are beset with pitfalls *actively* as well as happier accidents. Individuals tend, given similar circumstances, either to suffer passively or to oppose actively. For some, whether it is 'nobler in the mind to suffer the slings and arrows of outrageous fortune or to take arms against a sea of troubles and by opposing – end them' (Shakespeare, *Hamlet*) may consciously affect that decision. For others, it will be ease of comfort for themselves that will be the basis of their decision. It is of therapeutic importance, however, that some can only take the easy path while others feel they must strive always for perfection. If these factors are not fully conscious, if we can find no solution, then some help in understanding the difficulty may make them less compulsive, may provide freedom to react more construc- tively to events, whether good or ill, over which we have no practical control.

'I – he – she – we – seem to have lost interest in sex. Of course I know that first magic can never be expected to last but ...' 'Oh?? ...' say I, waiting for elaboration of how or why or when this particular person before me seems to have lost touch with a bit of themselves which was once so alive that it could be called magic, but which now, if not dead, is sleeping.

How tragically often I have heard these opening remarks in my professional life, both from my own patients and those of my colleagues. The precise phrasing may vary, but the assertion: 'Of course . . . always . . . never' is always there, as though the true delight of a good sexual relationship is known, as a fact, to have built-in obsolescence.

My 'Oh?' is of course the classic psychotherapeutic response, denoting interest, concern, willingness to hear more and to think on their behalf about things they cannot yet consciously recognize for themselves. But I do, in response to this particular, despairing inevitability, make sure that my question-mark is heard. *Why* should it never last?

How often has my 'Oh?' concealed a groan of despair. Not another! Can it be true? Perhaps most people find it really does just fade. Do I hope too much for them? But how often too I have found myself infected by a different feeling from a different patient, so that my 'Oh?' speaks for a part of them which is not prepared to suffer, which will fight and rage, if it can, and protest at those who 'all say' that passion fades. And with these people the question-mark in my 'Oh?' is saying 'Who says?' and 'Why shouldn't it last?' and 'I'll not just let it go without a fight.' For while this 'magic' may not easily or inevitably endure, it sometimes can, and much personal suffering and family instability could be avoided if it could last more often. Sexuality and its expression may not be the only or even the most important aspect of our ability to deal with life and each other, but it can enrich and cement relationships which are in trouble if it is marvellous, and can wreck otherwise good ones if it goes wrong.

Remember Linda (Chapter 1)? However mistaken her promiscuous path, however confused and immature her motives, she was without doubt a fighter. Doggedly, courageously even, she sought to find loving commitment through sex, and when she was helped to harness her sexuality, she succeeded. Yet for her parents' generation, this manner of quest was regarded almost unanimously as topsy-turvy, and sometimes, even today, it is widely believed in some cultures and groups that only after making a permanent emotional commitment can we expect to find sex free and enjoyable. Most religious bodies still hold, in theory, that full sexual expression must wait for marriage. Even those who include some sexual instruction in their pre-marital counselling seem to think that it is more important to agree on what curtains you will choose for your nest than to be sure that this most fundamental aspect of a relationship will work well between you. I have often heard those who advise the young say that the reason why some find sexual confidence awkward before marriage is because of their guilt, and that marriage will resolve this. Of course this may be true for many, and if it is, I would not expect to meet them. That the opposite is often true in that a lively sexual relationship seems actually spoiled by marriage, may be hard for those well-meaning people to credit. It does however account for a large part of our caseload for me and my colleagues.

With or without marriage, I have seen much unhappiness result from young people committing themselves too early. I met Louise when she was 23. Louise would seem to have been born with a silver spoon in her mouth. Not only were her parents loving and prosperous, they were also deeply concerned to understand the mores of their children's generation, and to offer their own example of behaviour standards and integrity without being prohibitive. They kept the lines of communication open with their daughter, who could consult her mother freely about sex and contraception. They listened, sometimes with difficulty and with earache, to the music of the time, aware that they must comprehend the philosophy of their young if they were to help them face a changing world in which parental authority was not to go unchallenged. Louise's contemporaries were genuinely and idealistically singing and 'talking about my generation' as though the future was positively in their hands. War would have been contrary to their humanitarian beliefs. However, they were not prepared passively to 'suffer': they were on the march. *Louise and Gerry: love dies, though friendship remains*

Part of Louise's idealism was a very positive new morality of sex and marriage. She saw it as 'giving' between her and the boy she first fell in love with in their last year in school. To withhold full loving and wait for engagement or marriage was in her view 'like prostitution of a very expensive kind: to sell sex for a promise to be kept for a lifetime in the style to which you hoped to become accustomed'. So she and Gerry made love fully from the start. On her mother's advice Louise took the pill without problems, having discussed thoughtfully that, until they were older and sure they wanted marriage, to bring a child into the world by accident would be irresponsible. They came to enjoy sex fully: their relationship blossomed and if it was other than 'love' that grew between them, I cannot find a better word. Their commitment was total and public, even blessed by both sets of parents, whose only reservation was that they were rather young to be sure that the relationship would last.

It is sometimes argued that the only trial of marriage is marriage, but those who 'live in' committedly are perhaps searching for the closest possible such trial, and it is sad when a couple experiences the obligation and duty of marriage without some of its undoubted benefits. Sadly, this proved to be the case for Louise and Gerry. Their relationship survived several years of partings, as Gerry went to university and found new friends and more importantly new interests, new parts of himself. Louise too found new challenges in her job and in travel: new aspects of herself emerged. Many of their new-found skills and interests were complementary and enriching. Both, for they were thoroughly lively and personable young people, met others who found them attractive, even flirted a little and were tempted further. Their love for each other survived these distractions. Each time they met again the first flush of reunion after separation made their loving as good as or better than ever – to begin with.

Yet once they were together again for a few days, they found they had less and less to say to each other. Their lovemaking became friendly, tender, unexciting. The anticipation of each parting would lead to a desperate clinging together, an increasing sense that they 'ought' to want each other and an increasing problem with spontaneity. As time went on, each reunion was dogged for each by a guilty sense of despair that the magic had gone. In their devoted longing to wish it were different, to struggle to recapture the wonder they once had, Louise found response more and more difficult. She began to fake orgasm. Gerry, knowing her so well even though he knew no other, was not deceived. Intercourse for him too became an effort, despite their continuing affection. I do not need to repeat here that erection cannot be made to order. In his fear of failure to please Louise yet again, Gerry's began to flag at the moment of penetration. Eventually their once lovely loving became an embarrassing routine. Although their friendship (which we notice in classical mores should have saved them, should have come first) lasted, their love died and they parted. It was a long time before either dared to love again.

Starting young as they did, Louise and Gerry at least had time on their side. With the general acceptance of living-in partnerships, we begin to see a whole new generation of women who choose this way of life. Until they want babies they do not opt for marriage, tending to wait until their careers are established, their 'fun', as sadly they so often put it, 'over'. They mean this in the sense of financial independence, freedom to travel and to buy their own flat. Rarely do they imply much in the way of sexual freedom to experiment with different relationships: their commitment and fidelity to their one man (or their man's to them) has at least the integrity and durability of a legal marriage. Indeed, some take it more seriously, bound, as they see it, by their freely given choice and freely given honour. Nevertheless – and I shall return to this in more detail in relation to the wish to conceive – when such a relationship does fail, a big chunk of both lives goes with it, and may require mourning and re-evaluation just as severe as that which accompanies the end of a legal marriage. One may perhaps give thanks that no children are to be torn and made unhappy, yet the part of the two separating selves which have come so far together, excluding all other, which will feel wasted unless the separation can be helped to be a learning experience, may be anguished indeed. We may speak grandly of growth through suffering. For a woman who, despite her other priorities, had hoped for children one day, and took for granted her brave new world of organized planning, to begin again at, say, 35 may take courage. Bitterness may be hard to avoid if the moment is lost.

Equally for the man, remembering how the disappointments and the tedium and restriction of a long-term, one-to-one relationship that has faded, remembering less easily the fun and the glory of the freely given early beginnings, may find it easier to revert to the charms, as recalled, of a bachelor existence than commit himself again. How many such men, envied and resented by their female contemporaries, are even now seeking to recapture their lost youth and dreams in a series of flirtations with younger women who find their maturer charms seductive, but who are themselves as yet in a different learning phase of development. I meet already some men for whom this envy may seem ill-placed before long. Flattered by the fantasy of sophistication created by having their pick of the pretty young girls, they struggle to adopt fashions and dances of a generation already ten years behind them, often incurring the scorn of those younger men who, in their own search for manhood, are all too ready to ridicule their ageing rivals.

One meets men of that generation who begin to hope for children at a time when their women are already wondering whether they have left it too late. Physically there is of course no reason why the men should not become fathers twenty years from now; and it may take less than that – ten perhaps – before their younger girlfriends have had all the fun *they* want. Out of many, I think particularly of one man. Forty now, squash-playing (though with increasing need for practice and work-outs and all the other trappings of the fitness fanatic), he sees his previous long-term girlfriend, who is 32, as too old for him. His new girl, at 23, is herself ambitiously enjoying her work in television, as well as the Bahamas holidays, the fast cars, that he can offer – at least in part because of the early struggles he and my patient survived together. I need not mourn for my patient, for I know her to have recovered from her bitterness and about to marry a man older in his turn, a widower, who is as keen for a family as she now is. But 'lover boy', as she now contemptuously calls him, still sees himself as a bright young playboy. His waistline is not thickening or his hairline thinning much . . . yet. He speaks often of the sons he will have 'one day', of teaching them to drive and to play rugger. They will not have the struggle he did, caused, as he sees it, by too early commitment. It is a sweet dream. The one factor he forgets to face is that if his first son were born tomorrow (and his new girl has plans to achieve her own programme before she will even consider marriage, so the biter is well bit), the teenager our friend has such high hopes of advising would by then have a father who is over sixty.

Lily: loss of inner privacy 'Ah, but', I can now hear a traditionalist cry, 'if Louise and Gerry and the others had been married, they would have had to stay together. They would have had to make a go of it.' Perhaps, and what kind of marriage it would have been we can never know. Lily and George did marry at a comparable stage of their relationship, and from her wedding night on, Lily told me, she never enjoyed sex again.

They were country people: Lily from a farmworker's family, apple-cheeked, plump, warm; George a production-line worker in the Midlands motor trade. The impression they gave of their early love-in-the-haystacks courtship made their present plight the sadder. They had been married several years now since their village wedding when both were 18, and had felt so much in love. All parents approved. Lily, like Louise, had felt her mother and father were not against sex, though 'officially' they said they should wait for marriage. 'They must have known mustn't they?' she said, smiling. 'I mean, they don't call it lovers' lane for nothing; they always egged us on.' During their courtship their love life had been exciting – idyllic, almost. The secrecy of it only added spice; but more than spice, it was 'all our own then; just him and me and the stars in the sky and the birds singing. Like a dream. Like the movies.'

Lily was devastated, and so was George, when on the first night of their honeymoon she found herself 'frozen'. They thought it might be the tiring journey and the shyness of checking into a seaside hotel. But no, the nights went by and they returned to the safety of their own little cottage and never again could Lily feel the earlier eagerness. Two clues emerged in talking. She remembered turning from the signing of the register and setting off radiantly down the aisle on George's arm, all the family and friends smiling, and 'I suddenly thought', she recalled, *'they know'* – and she had found herself blushing. To her surprise the expected bawdy earthy humour of the reception speeches, familiar as comfortable old shoes, had 'somehow not felt right', as though 'it was the lovely things we knew together they were joking about – as though we were public property now, and a rude joke at that'.

We may not be surprised that a clinic which sought to convey relearning techniques, following a session of group 'instruction' with sex films, was useless to Lily. The self-evident diagnostic blindness (that George's performance had not flagged; that these two not only knew how to do it wonderfully but knew how to do it together) in 'teaching' these two people to do it the 'standard' way – was the least of the insensitivity to the individuality of the problem. I had the advantage of hearing Lily say she 'wanted to come privately': her diagnosis in a nutshell, in more ways than one.

In this field 'private practice' can aptly describe the work and it is not simply about money. Understanding as I did, however, that it was the loss of her inner sense of the privacy of her own sexual desires which had interfered, it was easily possible to help Lily and George recapture something of the frame of mind which had felt 'private' before. They found their own game to play inside their heads: pretending they were meeting again and courting again for the first time, imagining the warm summer nights; the cool breeze between the trees; the scratch of the stubble beneath them . . . I fantasize – for the whole point was that they were to find again their *private* fantasy. That I should wish to hear or direct chapter and verse for them would be to miss the point as surely as the behavioural approach. Indeed my own chief gloom about Masters and Johnson's original studies of sexual performance in the laboratory is not that their results were consistent; for of course we may expect people in such carefully drilled circumstances to produce results that have much in common. It proves, for me, only that people function alike *in such circumstances.* And since neither I nor my patients have our love lives in such circumstances, nor do we plan to, the relevance seems limited. No, my worry is that because these results have led to such uncritical world-wide generalization from a very modest study, a 'treatment' regimen has been thrown up which is in danger of proving the coachability of mankind.

The   I shall return again to my criticisms of this piece of work.
behavi-   I do so reluctantly in a sense, for we cannot blame these
oural   two workers of integrity for the massive assumptions and
approach   misunderstandings which have been laid upon them by those therapists and patients who needed, clearly, so desperately to fasten upon what seemed like magic certainties in a field of human experience in which uncertainty is so threatening. Yet I must speak out, for in my experience the uncritical acceptance with which these modest laboratory experiments were greeted throughout the world has set back the clinical study of human sexuality by a generation. The therapeutic world fell upon them as manna from heaven, even though evident factual flaws must have been obvious to any woman who had had more than one orgasm in her life and known that they are never exactly the same. Every lover knows that orgasms not only feel different but are technically different with different touches, different pressures.

And what of those orgasms experienced in sleep; what of those which some people can only achieve by drugs; by bondage; by specific fantasy? To accept that because the orgasms of their experimental subjects were always achiev- ed by a certain movement, we could assume that this was the only mechanism for human orgasm, is patently ludicrous. This is obvious not only to a scientist but to anyone with minimal common sense, never mind any luck in the matter of loving. It is the nonsensical reception of this that we need to understand, all the more because 'science' increasingly depends upon making measurements rather than upon the findings of an inquiring mind.

When I contest the blind acceptance of these laboratory tests as a fact about human sexuality and contend that it sets back our knowledge by a generation, I am perhaps too harsh, for it did not stop 300 doctors in this country, nor others such as Helen Kaplan, from continuing to ask the question *why*. It did, however, give birth to a generation of 'therapists' who saw their task as telling their 'patients' how to run their lives; that athletic coaching was the appro- priate approach to sex and thus that human sex is a matter of athletics. It has taken ten years for those 'therapists' and those patients to reach the stage, as a colleague of mine from San Francisco put it, 'where Masters and Johnson left off and we' (of the Institute of Psychosexual Medicine) 'started 30 years ago': namely, asking simply why is it that some people need to be taught and why is it that individuals have not been able to trust their own instincts in this most indi- vidual aspect of personal expression.

I feel so strongly about this that I have digressed from Lily and George. They were not among those who proved 'coachable'. They were made of sterner stuff. We need to understand why Lily and so many like her react so suddenly and negatively to what one might expect would be a freeing occasion: the public blessing of her sexuality by her nearest and dearest. We cannot attribute her dramatic change to the forbidden fruits syndrome. It was for her, as another said of the same experience, 'as though I had literally turned off the light-switch of my own desires – and having done so could not find the way to reach back for it, to turn it back on'. The loss of a sense of privacy is only one factor, but it is a common one. How many young people find it impossible to enjoy their previously lively love-lives when for example they must share their parents' home? It is rarely as simple as fearing being heard through the bedroom walls, though many express it thus. For why should it matter? No, the pair of ears which 'might hear' is often to be found in the patient's own head: the 'good daughter' revived sometimes by geography, but often by what marriage, or even engagement, means in symbolic terms. Becoming a fiancée, becoming a wife, becoming a 'respectable old married woman', very commonly causes secondary sexual inhibition for girls for whom 'naughty' or 'secret' sex held nothing but confident delight.

Although Dorothy Parker drew our attention to the contrast between the hurly-burly of the chaise-longue and the deep peace of the double bed, and although we cannot ignore the importance of privacy and a home of their own for young couples, we must notice that it was of no help to Lily, and those who see the solution to such problems in terms of providing bricks and mortar alone will fail unless the need for privacy within the inner world is understood and dealt with also. Nor is it only women who can be thus affected.

Sam and Sarah: the inter- ference of parental blessing By the time I met Sam and Sarah they had not made love at all for almost seven years of their 11-year marriage, and it had been rare even before that, although they were other-wise happy and had three children. Neither of them had felt any sense of sexual delight in each other since the day they announced their engagement. Sam himself was as precise and as adamant about this as Lily. He could remember 'the very moment' when his sense of pride in his sexuality had 'turned off like a tap'. Now Sam was a good Jewish only son, of a warm if possessive mother and an easy-going father of modest means, a tradesman who had normal ambitions for their clever boy and took great pride in his hard work and academic achievement. They were delighted that these two good young people should find in each other such suitable mates. The parents became friends; there were even business advantages in the match. And, said Sam, he and Sarah were pleased that during their early courtship, both sets of parents encouraged them by tactfully leaving them alone. Whichever home they visited, they would be left together, to 'get to know each other'. They would make love eagerly, even in bed sometimes, but best of all on a family sofa or on the rug in front of the fire. They knew they would not be disturbed. Sam, inexperienced, was a bit inclined to premature ejaculation. Sarah did not easily reach orgasm with intercourse in these circumstances, but the whole business was tremendously exciting: she was readily orgasmic with play, he confident enough to try again with a second erection if there was time. And then, he said, the engagement was announced to everyone's delight, and from that moment on both sets of parents 'moved in'. They expected to sit together planning the wedding and would walk in on them at any time. It was never again enjoyable for either – 'as though', Sam said, 'our love life was their property now; as though they were watching us every minute'.

Sam and Sarah give us slightly more clue to the source of the prohibitive voice inside the head than do Lily and George, for many people can continue to flourish sexually despite their relationship being public knowledge. Some indeed can find the risk of interruption, of discovery, actually adds tension and excitement, increasing the confidence to make the most of very brief encounters. It was quite clear in Sam's view that it was not their sexuality but their marriageability which earned parental approval, and that the 'good son' in him was not the sexual lion or the rebel but the devoted worker, the 'good husband'. He was one of so many for whom these parts of ourselves are seen not simply as different and mutually enriching but mutually exclusive. It was necessary in treatment to help Sam see why for him, given the choice between these two parts of himself, it was the obedient son bit which should win and the rebellious lover which should go to the wall.

The obedient son

Once again, as with Lily's chance remark when telephoning for her appointment of her wish to 'come privately', it was Sam's very first words which gave me a clue. The doctor had made an appointment for me to see him and Sarah together, but Sam chose to *come on his own*. Sarah, he told me, had been to a doctor about her difficulties with orgasm some years earlier and had accepted the doctor's assessment that it was Sam's lack of experience that was the problem. You share with me the advantage of hindsight that this was clearly nonsensical; they had been much better eleven years ago when he was even less experienced! Nevertheless, we notice that Sam had believed it too, as

demonstrated by the fact that he was here before me, accepting responsibility not only for his own difficulties but for hers
too. Thus could begin some work to try to understand with
Sam that it was the obedient, self-blaming, wishing-to-please
aspect of him which was hindering his potency, and that this
had its roots, apparently in suddenly becoming a 'good son'
again rather than a secret lover.

Sarah's sexuality was not helped either when the relationship became public property. Why do so many find parental
blessing an interference? Whatever parents actually say or
believe, the common factor in my experience is to do with
the idea that parents – or indeed any respectable married
people – are not sexual people and don't have such ideas.
Thus for some, becoming that kind of person is incompatible
with being comfortably sexy. It is true in practical terms that
the more our energies are taken up with domesticity and
with the emotional demands of being a public partnership,
the less time and energy may be available for the romantic
lover. Some do manage; for some the different images are
not mutually exclusive, even though to switch personae from
the idealized domestic vision of the detergent advertisement
to that which is full of Eastern promise just because it is bed-
time may be easier for some than others! It seems clear that
for some, the feeling that wives or husbands or parents
cannot have a sexual life must come from an inner need to
block out the awareness of the sexuality of one's parents.

It is not easy for anyone to accept that parents have sexual
lives of their own; nor of course is it our business, any more
than our private sexual lives should be any business of theirs.
But some people can clearly manage to ignore these matters
and enjoy their private sexuality with or without any positive
blessing or encouragement from the parents themselves.
Others, it seems, need such positive blessing or 'permis-
sion', and if they cannot accept it from the parents they have,
they require it from a therapist. For others it seems to require
spelling out – 'we all know respectable mothers and fathers
are not like that' – before the individual can re-evaluate
whether they, in becoming a 'respectable parental figure' in
their own heads, need thus necessarily become asexual.

Sid: a good These details were not spelled out for Sam but another man
protective I may call Sid threw up a most vivid explanatory memory
lover which satisfied him at least as to the reason for his sudden

lack of enthusiasm. For Sid it was not engagement or even marriage which had made previously satisfactory sexual confidence disappear, but the unexpected illness of his much loved young wife. She was long since better, but Sid's confident potency had never fully returned, and it was clear between him and me that he had become protective towards Sue, so that the confidently aggressive aspect of his sexuality was in trouble. Wondering together why having to become a 'good' protective lover rather than a greedy selfish one had caused difficulties, he made a connection, to his surprise, with the first time he heard his parents making love, when he was about 14. It was around that time that he had begun to enjoy secret masturbation but he had not yet associated it with any knowledge or fantasy of the mechanisms of adult intercourse. 'I thought they were fighting,' he said. 'I sort of felt I ought to do something – to protect my mum – and yet at the same time I had this kind of excited feeling; not exactly knowing, but feeling it was something private, and not my business.'

It would have been interesting for me to pursue this association in detail, to establish precisely why reviving this memory should have freed Sid to recapture his sexual confidence. Because it did, it was not for me to suggest he return merely in order to satisfy my own intellectual curiosity. That for some it is the need to repress such prohibitive memories and for others the built-in certainty that grown-ups mustn't be sexual are but variations on a theme, or perhaps variations of degree. It does not seem necessary, either way, for such patients to accept a deep Freudian explanation. To see why they should operate so is often enough for them to dismiss their prohibitive inner voices and regain their sexual confidence. It is not, I believe, actual parental attitudes or behaviour that are as important at this level of understanding as the individual 'child's' ability to hear or be deaf, to accept or reject their own interpretation, real or imagined, of their 'child's role' towards their parents.

It is not always so simple. Zillah's frigidity since her marriage appeared at first sight to be an identical story to Sarah's or Lily's. How often even now I have to remind myself that my mind must remain open. How tempting it is, excitedly, to think, 'Ah, yes. I have heard this before. This is going to make another "case" like . . .' Zillah and her husband

Zillah: the terror of risking trust

Zach came from one of those Eastern Mediterranean countries where parents may still dictate a choice of mate from within their own religion and culture and where dissolution of any unhappy marriage is unthinkable. Zillah had, even so, received a Western education and had gained a psychology degree from an American university. She had had the freedom to explore the world before her marriage, and admitted that she had had earlier lovers and had enjoyed them. Zach knew this and accepted it, and their love-life together had been marvellous and growing better all the time – until their marriage.

It seemed that things began to go wrong on their return to the near East for the ceremony. They had had two children since but Zillah's severe secondary frigidity had now reached the point where she refused Zach always, and he was threatening to take a mistress. She was saying she wished he would, rather than face the guilt and misery of hating him even to touch her. I felt I was on sure ground here, and put it to Zillah that it was her own desires she was fighting. She accepted in theory that returning to a world in which women were not expected to have sexual needs might be the answer, but it was useless as far as helping her to recover her response. I noticed after several fruitless sessions that we spent most of our time arguing – she coming back at me with psychological theory. I realized then how difficult this independent young woman found it to trust herself to my care and to allow me to know best or to look after her.

Once we could share this perception we had found the key, for she was the same with her husband. The facts of that trip home emerged in a very different light. Mother's virtue was the least of the matter. It was the beloved Father who had devastated Zillah by revealing his feet of clay. He was planning to leave now that she was launched, to be with a girl nearer to her own age than her mother's. How bitter for a girl who had felt that he approved of asexuality and had idealized his daughter for her virtue. Her secret joy in her husband had been dashed because she became unable to trust 'these men' after all, or to trust her desires for them. Her husband was on the receiving end of an inner struggle with her trusting, man-loving self which was none of his making. Zillah began to review all this. There were further breakers ahead, for her sense of fidelity to her mother as well as her own betrayed sense of rivalry with this interloper clearly needed much exploration and airing. Perhaps the most interesting aspect for me, for it applies to so many, was that for Zillah what came across as healthy independence, a plausible and even intelligent refusal to allow me or her husband to 'take care of her', in fact proved a thin disguise for the terror of risking trust, once this trust had been, in her view, betrayed.

Zoe was another child of her time, nearing 40, with two lovely children and a successful career of her own. She was bright, chic and fiercely independent. But Zoe had not merely loved well and wildly and then lost it once – it had happened to her three times. Since she felt herself to be falling in love again she recognized, despite her wish to make a success of her marriage, that she was in some danger of repeating the pattern for a fourth time with perhaps really serious consequences, not just for herself but for those she loved. Zoe was another who had found the lively sexual relationship with her present husband begin to fade once they became engaged and deteriorated after the marriage. Interestingly, given her rational temperament, Zoe had stopped having intercourse for the period of her engagement. At the time she was not aware that she was 'going off him again', as she put it later, but rather made the deliberate choice to wait and 'save it up' for the wedding night, even though they had lived together joyously, riotously even, for 18 months before that. I have met many who so choose, and none of them has so far offered an explanation that can satisfy themselves.

Zoe: difficulty rivalling parents

It is of course a standard belief, a cliché almost, that men are more interested in the chase and the conquest than in the established relationship. Indeed many a mother or schoolmistress still warns her female charges that respect will be lost once they 'give in', and that all men want to marry a virgin whatever their own delight in sowing wild oats. In my experience this is by no means universally true. Even so, that women might themselves feel this way, and that it might even be a problem for some, is regarded as surprising and attributed, if so, to the 'dangers' of female independence. Maybe some, men particularly, find the alternative threatening. Yet clearly the feminine taste for the chase was a familiar idea even in the demure world of Jane Austen. Why should this be surprising? Zoe knew that,

despite feeling she had become 'bored' with her reliable
husband, she could not deny herself that she had become
equally bored, at least sexually, with the two men she had
loved before. She was too honest and self-aware to avoid
any longer the realization that this tendency was becoming
a habit; that the personalities of the men concerned could
not account for it, nor had any of them failed her sexually.
Why should she, like others we have discussed, find herself
unable to sustain sexual excitement once a man was, as it
were, hers?

I had a number of conversations with Zoe without
achieving much help in the revival of sexual response with
the partner she had. It does seem that once a relationship
has become entrenched into what one partner sees as
dullness, particularly if either has someone new and more
interesting around, it becomes *per se* more difficult to recapture the earlier magic in the way that proved so easy for Lily
and George, who were still both keen to do so. It is as
though the inner sense of boredom, dullness or respectability – however it may be defined for the individual –
becomes self-perpetuating. Any attempt to recapture the
sense of fun and sexiness seems the more inappropriate,
embarrassing and even improper. I have found myself
saying often: 'Perhaps we can free you to feel sexy again
even with your husband', or of course 'wife'. The Masters
and Johnson regimen is alleged to help here if both are sufficiently motivated, and still like each other enough. I can
imagine that it could remove the fear of failure as well as
the sense of impropriety.

Unfortunately, it had not worked for Zoe in the outpatient
setting, which was all there was available in this country.
Maybe the therapists, who, reasonably enough, had read
the American books and set out to try the method, were
themselves insufficiently skilled or trained in psychotherapeutic techniques to help it to work or to understand
when difficulty arose. Regrettably, even for consultant
psychiatrists or trained clinical psychologists, practical
experience of the unconscious 'transference' aspects of
individual therapy is not necessarily a large part of their
training, even today.

Zoe and her nice lawyer husband, who had himself had
a mild flutter with a girl at work in the face of Zoe's lack
of response, could not even begin with 'sensate focusing'
and the like. The relationship of 'brother and sister' which

their marriage had become, made even lying naked together to touch each other's faces seem inappropriate. Further, both were troubled by a feeling of 'infidelity' to their other partners which I find is surprisingly common even in the most light-hearted of affairs, if that affair has been sexually easier than the sexual life of the 'friendly' marriage. Zoe's new 'affair', we may notice, was at this stage mere fantasy; she had done nothing to express physically this new sense of having fallen in love yet again, this time with a totally unsuitable man. So for her at least, this sense of sexually 'belonging' not to the partner one legally has, but to the fantasy other, was a complex one. I have met men too — although Zoe's husband, still loving her most and wanting her more than his secretary, was not one of them — who find it impossible, improper, to think of their wives in such terms once they have found new excitement in another, even in fantasy.

Why should this be? As throughout this book, I draw no general conclusions, but for Zoe, and at least two others like her, there were several lines of investigation. At first we found ourselves discussing the thrills of the chase, the forbidden fruits, and the contrast between this frame of mind and that of the respectable public wife/mother figure who should not be sexy. This provided a possible explanation for her difficulties with marriage and with her previous engagement, and even with the fantasy wish that the new man might provide a renewal of the prohibited excitement. But we could not escape the fact that her second failed relationship, despite the added difficulty of daring to love again when the first had failed, could not be explained in this way. Here, it seemed, there was plenty of illicit excitement but the man's devotion, his wish to marry her, were he free, was in itself enough to remove the sparkle for Zoe. So we were back to Groucho Marx and the idea that perhaps any man who was at her feet became thereby diminished in her eyes. Again there was some logic here, but why should it hit Zoe's lively enjoyment of her own sexuality so hard that she should 'switch off' yet again, and again? Zoe, who was bravely honest with herself as far as she was consciously able, was the first to recognize that even were the new relationship to blossom, with all the cost to her marriage and children and career that would imply, she might well find the pattern repeated unless she and I could detect the source and review it. I cannot pretend that we did. She considered full analysis but I did not hear whether she pursued it. Another, with a similar history, left both her husband and treatment. They did however reveal a common story, as have several others, from which we may at least speculate that something happened to them psychologically which had similar roots to that which happened to Zillah.

Zoe's father adored her and revelled in her brightness and her success and was protective to her sexually, as was Zillah's father. Neither was in any doubt that as far as Father was concerned, these were the talents he appreciated; that their fathers, at least as they saw it, would not find it too easy to bless their sexuality toward men of their own. We have no evidence to suggest that the fathers of either Zoe or Zillah actually sexualized, even unconsciously, their love for their daughters, and it may well be that for these two at least, the daughters' sense that their 'hearts belonged to Daddy' came from within themselves. Other fathers may actually, in their devotion or excitement in their pubescent daughters' emerging sexuality, play into this by over-protectiveness; by being, quite unwittingly, intense in their difficulty in knowing and envying their daughters' interest in boys.

The influence of fathers Still other fathers go so far as to express these feelings sexually in active incestuous activities with their daughters, causing deep and complex disturbance. Such incestuous activities are reported quite often, sometimes in fantasy but often in fact in otherwise respectable families. One can only speculate about the actual incidence but the gathering evidence suggests that it is more widespread than previously thought. With the woman as a patient, I have usually found myself needing to examine the daughters' own deep sense of guilt, certainly repressed since they were clearly the 'innocent' parties at the time, that they had somehow unwittingly invited their father's (or other older male relative's or 'assaulter's') interest and may have been unconsciously excited as well as dismayed and frightened by it. Thus the burden of ill-understood shame, guilt, infidelity to Mother, remains to interfere with guilt-free sexual enjoyment when adult, with a man of her own, for her own pleasure. Even when such emotional entanglements are quite unconscious and in no way acted out, I notice that it seems often to be the most respectable of fathers — those who would be horrified at the mere suggestion that they found some excitement in their daughters' sexuality — who in their unconscious struggle with this 'disgraceful' bit of themselves, send out over-protective and over-prohibitive messages which play into the uncertainty of their daughters. It is as though they find themselves protecting their daughters, unconsciously, from their own shameful wishes most of all. Often such men have frigid wives. Often, too, the increasingly tense father and daughter relationship reinforces the daughter's normal developing sense that her interest in men, as represented by her father, must be guilt-ridden as it involves inescapably rivalry and infidelity towards her equally loved mother.

Unlike Zillah's mother, Zoe's was herself a bright, beautiful and talented career woman. Thus Zoe's experience that these were the aspects of herself that gained her father's approval were heavily reinforced. Her own mother, and her husband's devotion to her, was living proof that this was the 'right' kind of woman to be. Zoe had, less than consciously, devoted her life to becoming this kind of 'approved' woman, and with great success. Since she and her mother loved each other with mutual pride, the sense of rivalry between them had posed no major problem and had never needed to become conscious. We may remember Zillah's shock when her idealized father, whom she 'knew' loved 'good girls', revealed his sexual liking for a rival of her own age, sexy, and thus far from 'good'. There was not such scandalous trauma for Zoe, but we heard that, in fact, her sister was very different from her: idle, flirtatious, irresponsible, and interested only in clothes, music and boys. Her parents, Zoe felt, loved this envied rival 'at least as much' as they did Zoe. They never showed serious disapproval of her, and defended her if Zoe, in her wish for some justice, drew their attention to the contrast between her sister's minimal efforts to be the kind of girl they 'wanted' and her own lifetime dedication and wish to please.

What has all this classic 'Electra' interplay to do with Zoe's problem? I shall return to it again, for clinical experience does justify over and over again its importance in the development of confident sexuality in women, as does the comparable Oedipal struggle for men. It became clear between us that for Zoe and others, sub-conscious rivalries with Mother and sister had made it very important for these women to be reassured that they were 'the best'. Such reassurance was gained for Zoe at least by the 'conquest' of a new man — by that tremendous lift which sexual admiration gives that people really are, for those moments at least, totally desirable, totally approved, 'chosen' above all others. But once achieved, this feeling began to seem hollow, perhaps even prohibited.

I have met men for whom the same seems to happen, and we need to acknowledge the great difficulty, as with nature's battle between young stags and the head of the herd, of rivalling parents without guilt. It is a fundamental element of growing up which accounts for many sexual difficulties, both primary and secondary, and may disable the struggle for success in other aspects of life. There is pain, as well as pleasure, not only for the ageing proud father but for the emerging son too, when he begins consistently to beat his father at games; the more so if it was a loving proud father who taught him in the first place. A successful businessman whose father, of humble achievements, boasts of him constantly, ran into quite deep emotional confusion when he found that he was not actually loved for his success by his colleagues at work. Confronted for the first time with the conscious awareness of rivalry, resentment, hatred and the envy of his colleagues, this man was devastated at a level which he found incomprehensible. Later, he told me, public-school idealist that he was, 'They say for success in business you have to look English; think Yiddish. My tragedy is that I'm the other way round.' Neither of us seriously believed that anti-Semitism was a fundamental cause of his dismay, for he had come to terms with that long ago. The feeling that he 'ought' to be a second-class citizen compared with his loved father however was revived by the discovery that some of his colleagues could envy and hate rather than praise him for his achievements.

There is a story about Freud which may be apocryphal but is, I understand, factually documented. Much of Freud's thinking is currently criticized as some of his original ideas are developed. It was his genius that observed that, in listening to his patients when they faced away from him, they invested him with thoughts he did not have. Thus his concept of the unconscious was postulated. Many have since been able to explore futher and build on the foundations he laid. We may remember that this man from an orthodox Jewish background became aware of his feelings towards his father and somehow associated them with the Old Testament 'God the Father', and assumed his atheistic theory from there. The story goes that towards the end of his life, Freud the son went up to a mountain top, and realized, reflecting, that he had been a more successful man, had achieved more in his life, than had his father . . . And then he fainted!

10

Contraception: unconscious factors

Methods and their meaning
Valuing femininity
Clitoral orgasm: the real thing?
Vasectomy

Motiva-
tion for
contracep-
tion
Few medical topics have received such world-wide large-scale statistical study as the relative efficiency of contraceptive methods. It is inevitable, however, that such studies are based on the assumption that the patient is merely a physical body governed by a wholly rational mind, and that the doctor is making equally objective physical and rational observations. It is not our task to question such figures. They are crucial, other things being equal, to the quality of advice we may give our patients.

However, it is important to recognize that when the measuring instrument, the doctor, is equipped to observe unconscious factors a surprisingly different assessment may be made. This crucial variable affects significantly, in many cases, the motivation to contraceptive effort, the choice of method and the efficiency with which the individual patient is able to use such methods. Insistence upon, rejection of, or difficulty with a particular method may be yet another way in which a patient may reveal underlying sexual anxiety. The method must suit the individual and his or her partner if it is to be effective in the long term.

Should we be surprised that some men as well as some women find themselves less interested sexually without the 'sporting chance' of pregnancy? Many women find difficulty in enjoying sex when any effective contraceptive method is used, in spite of their certainty that they do not wish to conceive. It often appears that such women have grown up to feel that sex, possibly parental sex, was an acceptable idea only for the propagation of the species. Such patients who feel, unconsciously, that the right purpose of intercourse is conception may experience difficulties with any serious contraceptive effort.

Pauline complained of loss of orgasm with the cap. *Pauline:* Examination revealed that she also had no enthusiasm when *the pill* the sheath had been used previously and that she could now *can be* only tolerate intercourse at about the time of ovulation. *safe* Suggestions that the pill might be better for her produced the reaction, 'It is too safe'. She revealed that she had only enjoyed intercourse to the full when they were trying for each of her three children. She had on each occasion found orgasm impossible after her first missed period until she had finished feeding each of the babies. Her own mother had been very close and protective to each of her own three children, but the patient had the impression from her that sex for its own sake was an improper and prohibited desire. Interpretation of these difficulties enabled the patient to begin to enjoy intercourse again, regardless of the method chosen.

A similar emotional pattern may directly affect the *Patricia:* efficiency of a particular method. Patricia was an efficient, *uncons-* atheist mathematician who was constantly changing her *cious* mind about taking the pill, and was thus frequently at risk *doubts* through irregular cycles and medications. This behaviour *about* seemed totally at odds with the rational, competent image *sexual* that she presented. Psychological exploration revealed a *desires* childhood with parents who were always abroad and a correspondingly deep feeling for the values of the nuns who taught her and provided her closest loving relationships. Intellectually, she totally rejected Roman Catholicism and yet, emotionally, each renewed religious controversy brought to the surface unconscious doubts about the rightness of her sexual desires while using contraception. Interpretation and insight enabled her to come to terms with this. She was then able to enjoy intercourse and take the pill efficiently.

Difficulties may arise for women who begin to take responsibility for the contraceptive method, whichever female method is chosen. Such a patient may insist that all is well in this respect but will produce other symptoms to draw attention to herself while disguising that she has an emotional problem.

Penny:
distasteful
excitement
of sperm

Penny attended a family planning clinic for a year for her pills and had attended for a cap for two years previously. During this time she had become friends with members of the clinic staff as she had a bright, helpful manner. The doctor always found her quite charming. They would discuss their children and the local arts club, in which both were interested. It took these three years for the doctor to notice that, although clinically 'everything was fine', the patient had tried three different caps and three changes of pill. Always it was, 'Yes, it suits me beautifully, it's just that I have these blinding headaches' or 'this continual bleeding'. Her inability to complain and be an ordinary patient was the measure of her difficulty in owning to needs or problems. When the doctor finally observed that no method they tried seemed very satisfactory but that she did not seem to dare to complain, the patient was able to reveal angrily her resentment that her husband no longer had the responsibility. Intercourse could then be discussed more freely and the patient tearfully admitted that she found his sperm messy and distasteful. With the sheath and coitus interruptus she had been spared this and had enjoyed intercourse to the full; with female methods she hated it. To her, intercourse, both sexual and social, needed to be 'nice' — all sweetness and light. Put in touch with the underlying, distasteful excitement in this concept of 'nasty mess', and the associated resentment at receiving sperm, she was able to reach orgasm again without reverting to male methods.

Many patients are able to confess to such feelings in the context of a doctor–patient relationship that allows discussion of what is to them a very delicate and embarrassing matter. It is tempting to blame lack of enthusiasm for sex on the pill and to feel that the explanation is hormonal. With increasing experience in exploration of the patient's feelings, we find that 'hormonal frigidity', which does seem occasionally to occur despite deep scrutiny, is the exception rather than the rule.

In the case of Polly, a middle-aged patient, a clue to the idea that the obvious hormonal explanation would not suffice was detected by the fact that she implied the doctor should suggest to her husband that they should 'ease up' at their age. She revealed great unease about her own sexual excitement now that her children were reaching sexual maturity. The maximum efficiency offered by the pill was vital to her lest pregnancy should reveal that she still had a sexual life. But her husband's emission inside her, never before experienced, was too exciting. Her mounting feelings were switched off in panic at their height, leaving her with disappointment and frustration, which she reported as 'disgust'. Interpretation of her need to feel allowed to continue to enjoy her sexual life was sufficient for her to resume orgasm, despite the pill. Incidentally, she changed in appearance from a rather scruffy, depressed middle-aged frump into a well-groomed, cheerful person looking ten years younger. She took a part-time job to help pay for redecorating the house and her relationships were transformed, not only with her husband but with her teenage daughter who had had behaviour problems. The mother no longer resented her emerging sexuality, and the girl's school performance improved.

Polly: unease as children reach sexual maturity

Some women can enjoy sex when their men take contraceptive responsibility, but not when they have to use something more reliable themselves. It seems they could enjoy it with their man 'in charge' of contraception and of initiating sexual love — as it were despite themselves. It is as though to respond joyfully to a man's desire is easier than to go seeking pleasure themselves. Even the regular swallowing of a pill could produce this feeling that they are 'looking for it' and 'making themselves available'. This can be enough to revive prohibitions and interfere with confident arousal.

Allison had enjoyed a rich and joyful marriage with three babies planned successfully with the sheath and vaginal orgasm experienced nearly every time. An obstetric difficulty prompted the necessity for maximum efficiency — the combined pill. From that moment she had no orgasm and her eagerness for intercourse had rapidly dwindled until after nine months it was non-existent. Inquiries about feeling the risk of pregnancy to be important to her drew a blank,

Allison: response possible when husband was in charge

as did various changes of prescription. Eventually the doctor noticed that she was having to make all the suggestions without cooperation, and related this to the way the patient spoke of her once so splendid husband. He had been ill, demoted at work, and was no help around the house. Understanding of this resentment enabled the patient to admit her difficulty in taking responsibility — for practical decisions about the family and contraception, and for her own sexual desires also. The pill, simple and unpremeditated though it is, was enough to make her feel too responsible for intercourse. She had grown up with the idea that sex was for men. When her husband was in charge with the sheath, she could respond to the full, as it were despite herself. With the idea that she was entitled to pleasure for her own sake out in the open, she was able to resume orgasm. Her husband soon found a better job under the influence of her return to sexual responsiveness!

The con- In the early days when the diaphragm was the only
traceptive method for women who wanted to take their own respon-
diaphragm sibility for planning, some of them were in real trouble. For the diaphragm requires quite positive forethought and action, sometimes too difficult for those who have inhibitions about touching the vagina. Many women find this side-effect-free method perfectly acceptable and can insert it as one said, 'when I hear the click of the gate', and find it fun as part of their own pleasurable anticipation, long forgotten by the time love-making gets underway. But those who are unhappy with it, either because they have been poorly taught how to insert it and check it, or because it evokes for them these 'disgraceful' feelings of messiness or naughtiness — not only of the physical process but of the desires which accompany them — are far more likely to leave it out unless they are very sure love-making will take place. They find themselves having to say 'excuse me' at what should be a magic moment, to rush off to a cold bathroom and struggle with the contortions of inserting a slippery cap that can spring from the fingers like an orange pip. No wonder that if they return to bed to find the moment gone, it may be easier not to bother. Diaphragms, though effective in confident hands, do not afford any protection from within the bathroom cupboard.

In the matter of choice of method, it is often the case that **The IUD**
the presented difficulty may be directly related to the nature
of the problem. An exaggerated instance of reluctance to
take responsibility for intercourse, for contraception, and
for her own desires is sometimes met with in the patient
who insists upon an intra uterine device (IUD). With this
method, of course, the patient literally has to do nothing
for herself. The device is inserted by someone else and she
does not have to think about it at all. We have met patients
like this who refuse to take responsibility in other aspects
of their life. Often the doctor finds herself having to do all
the work without any response from the patient, and is then
not surprised to hear that the husband at home is put in
the same position.

While the IUD does, in some cases, cause heavy and
painful periods or intermenstrual spotting for purely
physical reasons, it is noteworthy that patients vary very
much in their reaction to this, as they do in their reaction
to the side-effects of other methods. There are patients who
will willingly put up with these difficulties for the sexual
spontaneity conferred. Others may complain bitterly about
their heavy and painful periods and, in response to sensitive
interpretation, may reveal the resentments they feel about
their responsibility for intercourse. Again, it is not surprising that a woman who sees intercourse for her husband's
pleasure alone, and resents this, is more likely to 'suffer'
from side-effects than one who can see such methods as a
small price to pay for her own pleasure and fulfilment.

But if a woman, having had all the babies she wants, feels
that a sporting chance must remain and that she is not
emotionally ready to put up the shutters of her fertility by
sterilization or hysterectomy but nevertheless dislikes the
hassle of the cap, then the forgettable IUD, fitted by
someone else, may be appropriate and well worth the
longer, heavier period. Conversely, an IUD may be less
advisable for a woman who has already suffered risk to her
fertility through a tubal pregnancy or infection. Although
she may insist that no other method will do, how much
better if she can be helped to understand her difficulty in
making the positive commitment required to use a method,
such as the pill, that may be safer for her.

Some women worry continuously about what a pill may
be doing to their body, exchanging the fear of pregnancy
for the fear of dying, while others feel it has transformed

their lives. Despite the known risks I have heard of women who have been so terrified of losing the benefits to their love-lives of the certainty it provides, that they have gone so far as to lie to their doctors about such danger signs as an inflamed vein or swollen leg; have acquired pills from other sources if he refuses them, without regard for whether the same prescription might be suitable, rather than part with the method they see as indispensable to their sexual happiness.

Such extreme attitudes may well have an emotional explanation. Just as people are rarely hateful on purpose, they are rarely wilfully stupid on purpose. For people with a reasonably confident, mutually tolerant and humourful sex life, any method of contraception should be suitable and we may help them choose on purely practical and medical grounds. Conversely, if they have difficulty with one method or another, and there are good medical and practical reasons why that method is wise for them, we may approach the matter from the opposite end and attempt to understand with them why their less than conscious emotional prejudices may make it difficult.

An effective contraceptive method does not merely prevent conception. If that were the only consideration, abstinence would be suitable. Contraception is, by definition, for people who wish to avoid pregnancy as well as having an active heterosexual love-life. It must therefore aim to encourage that love-life to be spontaneous, carefree, enjoyable. If it does not succeed in this, the chosen contraception will ultimately be left in the cupboard, in the pocket or in the packet. Indeed if those who seek to aid population control in less affluent communities fail to convey that contraceptives are aids rather than hindrances to this human aspect, rejection may be inevitable.

We have met patients who blame the sheath for their lack of enjoyment, and who on further examination blame their husbands. The idea that they could do something about intercourse in order to make it better was foreign to them. They needed to see the difficulty as outside themselves. The concept of penis-envy was considered when looking at Fiona's problems (Chapter 7). We have come to see it not as a primary difficulty but rather as a defensive system against a deeper difficulty about the implication of being a woman.

Peggy appeared to be rather tough and matter-of-fact, *Peggy:*
revealing resentments of her husband's orgasm, which she *learning*
saw as better than her own. She complained also that she *to value*
wished he would spend more time on her and less upon *femininity*
the car, and was able to accept the interpretation that she
felt the same about his technique in intercourse. In
understanding that she seemed to feel that men always had
the best of it, the patient recalled that she had always been
a tomboy as a child, feeling boys' toys and games to be more
exciting than girls'. She believed that her parents had really
wanted a boy rather than a girl. The doctor proceeded to
put her in touch with the idea that being a woman was good
and valuable in its own right, and the patient began to
understand why she valued herself, her feelings and her
vagina so little. She began to dress and behave in a more
feminine fashion, and to see her vagina not as a poor
substitute for a penis but as a valid organ of feeling in its
own right. Her fantasy was that feminine feeling, if uncontrolled, would be foolish, laughable and vulnerable. To see
that a competent adult, the doctor, could value such aspects
of herself was enough to give her confidence to reveal her
feelings to her husband in intercourse, abandoning those
defensive control systems which are so fatal to the achievement of feminine orgasm.

We have discussed earlier how some patients' capacity for *Clitoral*
orgasm seems, before therapy, to depend upon one method *orgasm —*
of contraception or another, or upon whether they are trying *the real*
to become pregnant. For many patients orgasm is easy by *thing?*
clitoral stimulation, but they feel something is missing or
that this is not the real thing. The penis in the vagina does
not, however, for them produce a sensation that leads to
orgasm. They may feel that there is no feeling there at all,
or that their desire and excitement are 'switched off' at the
moment of penetration.

Masters and Johnson [3] have shown with apparent
conclusiveness that, in physical terms, vaginal orgasm is
produced by a the stimulation of the clitoris by the action
of the penis. We can say confidently however that, quite
apart from the totally different physical sensation, in
emotional terms, stimulation of the clitoris by petting and
the orgasm thus produced is a different experience
psychically from the experience of orgasm brought about

by the penis in the vagina. The togetherness, mutual abandonment of control systems, the emotional acceptance of the penis and all it implies in terms of the man, and of the vagina and all it implies in terms of the woman, make this a unique experience that is not mimicked emotionally by mutual masturbation, however loving. It is emotionally more difficult for many people, and many who cannot achieve it know that they are missing something. Equally, many who can achieve it are in no doubt as to its importance or as to the difference.

In many cases putting a woman, who has hitherto only enjoyed orgasm through clitoris, in touch with her vaginal sensation by using well-tried psycho-physical techniques may be very useful. One often finds the opportunity to draw attention to the emotional/physical parallel in that, as her sensation is chiefly on the outside, so may her sexual feelings be chiefly superficial also. Clitoral sensation is usually experienced and learned early, whether the pleasure is guilt-ridden or not. Vaginal sensation does need to some extent to be learned to be appreciated, even in the absence of emotional prohibition. Having recognized her difficulties and shared them with the doctor, a woman will, in coming to accept for herself the concept of the vagina as a touchable acceptable organ of pleasure with its own erogenous pressure areas, also comes to accept its sensations and her own desires as permissible and exciting.

However, when patients complain that orgasm can be brought about by digital stimulation of the clitoris only, which must be by definition outside the act of intercourse itself, deeper difficulties may be encountered. Again the concept of penis-envy may be helpful in the understanding of such patients.

The concept implies a woman's feeling of being a second-class sex, lacking this brave organ, the symbol and instrument of potent manhood, the penis. Unconsciously, she envies the man, the organ, and all it represents, and reacts against him with resentment, anger and the need to control or to destroy. We have met patients who felt this way, and who, if not wholly frigid, have enjoyed only clitoral pleasure. Some have said they always felt a boy was a better thing to be than a girl, or that their parents always wanted a boy. Others have, in their aggressively controlling life-pattern, like Brunhilde, seen their love-life as a battle to be won [1], but have been saddened by the destructive effect of their winning.

In the present context it seems that for them the separate, individual orgasm of mutual masturbation is easier than orgasm within intercourse. A little more of themselves is controlled and held back or, conversely a little more of the man is controlled and kept out. Orgasm within intercourse implies a total abandonment of these controls; a total acceptance not only of the vagina and of the female emotions associated with it, but also of the penis and all it emotionally implies in terms of the relationship to a man. The absence of this totality of sharing and mutual acceptance may have disastrous effects upon the relationship for many people. Husbands feel less than fully loved and accepted, while wives, in their disappointment, become resentful or blaming.

Rosemary, a young bride of 18 months came for a cap check and complained that she could not enjoy intercourse itself, having earlier enjoyed mutual masturbation to the full. She had now reached the state when she could not bear her husband to touch her at all. She confessed that she felt very masculine and was worried about homosexuality since she was becoming interested in the idea of men together, and was also obsessed by horror films and death, finding all these ideas both repugnant and fascinating. She felt her husband was defective in something which should stimulate her clitoris in intercourse, but hated the sensation of the penis inside. She had masturbated in adolescence and would have hated her mother to know — and yet would have liked to shock her. *The vulner-ability of vaginal orgasm*

This patient was extremely controlling in the interviews, but during interpretations was put in touch with the excitement underlying all these repugnant feelings. She began to complain less of her husband and to discuss the fears underlying the need to keep control. Her sexual, passionate feelings would shock people. The doctor was not shocked, and the patient could see that it was she herself who felt the idea shocking. Then she was able to face the idea that she might be really 'showing herself' in vaginal orgasm — violated, exposed, wide-open and vulnerable. At the next visit vaginal orgasm had been achieved and the patient was radiant and delighted. Her husband, she confessed proudly, had danced round the room with delight, and she could confess that she had always found the penis exciting but had felt ashamed to admit it.

For patients who feel that the penis is a necessary pre-requisite of true sexual pleasure, the clitoris is indeed a poor substitute. We find that the necessary focus of therapy is once again the patient's attitude to the vagina; the exploration of the feeling of its inadequacy, nastiness, unimportance, or vulnerability; followed by the encouragement to value it not as a second-class substitute for a penis but as a valid organ of total feeling in its own right. In parallel with these bodily attitudes goes the emotional corollary. The idea that woman is the second-class sex, that female capacities and female desires are poor imitations of the male, is explored. The idea is then encouraged that to be a first-class woman is a richer and more fruitful aim than to be a second-class man.

An important conclusion has been suggested by Dr Main as the result of our consistent findings, and has been repeatedly confirmed in this study. The implication of Freud's work is that penis-envy is a primary difficulty. We have found consistently that the syndrome itself may be interpreted. It is our conclusion, therefore, that penis-envy, with its wish for or resentment of manhood, is not a primary difficulty but rather a defensive system against the greater difficulty of being a woman.

Vasec-tomy: physically 'nothing'? Before vasectomy became an option, those couples for whom the man took responsibility for contraception, with condoms or coitus interruptus, did not need to consult doctors. By the late 1960s, however, many patients were either considering vasectomy or had already undergone the operation. Most of these were happy well-adjusted couples who had achieved all the pregnancies they wished, and had thought the matter through together. We found the procedure did them no harm and they were happy with the result, although a few complained that they had not been warned that some bruising and discomfort might follow. As it became fashionable, the idea was bandied about that it was physically 'nothing', and for most men that was true. The unlucky ones, however, felt somewhat betrayed if they had, for example, to take a few days away from work with the public explanation and teasing that was evoked. This was similar to the disappointment of high expectations women had of childbirth in the early days, as now. Why is it that it is so difficult to be truthful with patients? Why do we expect it to be helpful if medical practitioners and their colleagues give false reassurances to people in their care?

Before recommending the permanent step of vasectomy we were alert for emotional danger signals. We wondered why, for example, some men should insist on being sterilized, or some of their wives insisted it should be the man, when generally speaking it was the woman who felt she would not want to 'go through' further child-bearing no matter what family disaster might befall. One often offered answer was that sterilization for the women was a bigger, more dangerous operation. With laparoscopic sterilization becoming more readily available, this argument lost some of its force, and although the marginal risks of general anaesthesia had to be taken into account, there were those men who preferred this to being operated on under local anaesthetic. Once again, as in our past studies, we found ourselves interested in those couples whose request for vasectomy might not be quite as reasonable as it seemed. Would we find, we wondered, that this was sometimes a 'visiting card' for people with emotional or sexual problems, readily treatable by psychosomatic methods, but certainly not by surgery? Could we learn to foresee in advance which patients would be trouble-free and which might have emotional or sexual problems afterwards? And if so, could we be sure of avoiding this, by developing better counselling skills?

Twelve of us arranged to meet together regularly under the leadership of Tom Main. We made a three-month pilot study in which doctors reported cases 'of interest'; those who revealed problems [8,9,10]. At the end of that time enough clues had emerged for us to construct an observation form on which we could fill in our comments before subjecting them to computer analysis. We then recorded the next 20 couples requesting vasectomy that we met, thus avoiding the temptation to select 'interesting cases', and between us, we had 200 couples to study quite quickly. A year later we followed them up.

Most of our patients knew what they had wanted from the operation and had got it. Those for whom fear of further pregnancy or difficulty with other contraceptive methods had interfered with their confident sexual enjoyment found great relief, so much so that many became quite evangelical about it, recommending it to all their friends! We did begin, however, to notice a rather similar phenomenon to that of men being expected to attend births: that it might be seen as cowardly or irresponsible not to do so. If a whole police station or fire station or golf club went 'vasectomy mad', it might be the very one who was too uncertain of himself to be the odd man out who would have his potency shaken by the operation. I remember one such man telling me ruefully later, 'I nearly got up and ran when the surgeon said, ''That's one side done, laddie'', but I didn't even have the guts to do that! Why oh why do we worry so much about making fools of ourselves!'

We were not surprised, for it was familiar ground for us, to meet, from the start, a few of those couples for whom the wife had difficulty with enjoyment if having to use contraceptives herself, so that her husband felt obliged to do so. This did not necessarily imply a serious problem if it was simply a matter of the man wanting, as one put it, 'to be shot of the French letter, which really is, as they say, a bit like bathing with your boots on'. But if a wife's true frigidity was revealed in discussion, it was clear that vasectomy would not solve her difficulties in itself, so that, even were the operation to proceed, attempts were made to help her achieve pleasure should she wish, whatever method of contraception was decided.

It was a new experience for us, however, to find that there were men who took charge of contraceptive matters, not at their wives' behest but because they themselves insisted. Some we met seemed to feel this for protective reasons, and we detected ideas that contraception, like pregnancy and sex, were seen by them as potentially damaging for their wives, who had already, they felt, 'been through enough'. Some of the wives saw it this way too, thereby putting pressure upon their husbands, however willing, to take their share of 'suffering'. That was fair enough, but with some couples, whose love-lives were less than rewarding because of this very set of beliefs, we found it wise to have these motivations open and clearly understood between them. An attitude which perceived not only childbearing and contraception but sexual love too in terms of women 'suffering' so that a good man would wish to 'spare' her, could become self-fulfilling, creating a truly suffering, angry, castrating wife, with a placating self-blaming husband. Vasectomy was a predictable step in the history of such a relationship, practically sensible perhaps, but providing no help to the underlying joyless vision of their sexual roles.

These people needed help at another level and a minor surgical procedure was not likely to provide the solution. Some indeed, hoping for magic from vasectomy, found afterwards that their marital discord was nakedly revealed and the more painfully resented for the failure of the hoped-for miracle. A well-meaning husband had 'suffered' too — and for nothing.

Other men, who had always needed to be in charge, and for whom vasectomy was a logical final step, seemed to have their own inner difficulties in trusting their women, or in trusting themselves to them. Some feared that the woman (arising, it seemed, from their relationship with their mothers yet again) would 'swamp them' should they relax their defensive vigilance for a moment. For others the reverse side of the coin seemed more relevant. They had felt over-responsible for mother and thus for all women, fearing that their wives might be damaged should they have to fend for themselves, and should they fail to protect them. One such man revealed clearly to me that it was his own unconscious resentment of this 'mother' (his wife) who had turned her affections to his rivals, their children, which he needed to protect her against most of all. No, not quite most of all. His need to protect *himself* from knowing that he had dreadful, murderous feelings within him towards someone he loved, was his most serious problem of all. His was a deep and difficult secondary problem. Most of the men that we met in the vasectomy study vividly revealed similar attitudes without any serious effects upon love-lives which had muddled along well enough until then, and would continue to do so whether either partner were sterilized or not. We were observing merely the rich variety of human nature, and learning something of the less conscious under-currents upon which we so often base what we see as perfectly local decisions.

One lively example amused us all. The man was a naval petty officer, accustomed to responsibility and command. His doctor described him as 'a handsome beefy hulk'. His wife sat 'cowering' beside him, silently, 'like a frightened mouse'. He told the doctor that he had always 'been careful' (a common English euphemism for withdrawal or coitus interruptus). He was, he said, very good at it. They only had five children and one or two of the 'mistakes' ended in miscarriage, and of course he was away at sea a lot! He was now going to have a vasectomy, and then asking the doctor kindly to sign the form forthwith, that was to be that. Now the doctor, her back to the wall, reminded herself that she was supposed to be doing good joint counselling here, and this overpowering man was making it very difficult for her or his wife to get a word in. She swung round in her swivel chair so that her back was to him and said to his wife, 'And how do you feel about all this?' As the mouse blinked, and opened her mouth to speak for the first time, her husband slammed his fist down on the desk. 'She thinks', he shouted, 'that it's a good idea!'

With another couple it was the glamorous wife who controlled the interview, by 'playing', her doctor said, 'the sweet little thing'. Fluttering her eyelashes, giggling and patting her husband's hand, she was telling the world of 'all she had been through' and how wonderful it was of her handsome husband to be prepared to make this sacrifice for her. The doctor found herself irritated by this, feeling, she said, that the husband was 'so good-natured, such a dish, that he should be allowed to father a thousand children if he wished!' Yet their love-life was good and remained so after the operation. Whatever the doctor's prejudices against this 'poor little' woman wrapping such a lovely man round her little finger, it was clear that the husband lapped it up and really did feel privileged to be making this 'sacrifice' for his beloved.

We met a few too where the marital warfare was cold, entrenched and unconscious. Though we could not prevent these couples from proceeding to vasectomy, we tried to allow them to share their pain, to be warned that the operation would change nothing. Some angry disappointed wives seemed determined to 'get him done' as if in punishment for 'his' sins of omission in failing to give sexual fulfilment. Some of the men, too, were determined to 'get themselves done' — sometimes positively in fearful submission, sometimes in 'downing tools' passive aggression, sometimes in a kind of tooth-sucking 'Right then', as if to say 'That'll show her.'

Then there were those who were looking, it seemed, for a 'final solution', with all the sinister overtones that phrase has. To what? To uncontrolled or disappointing fertility perhaps, or to sexuality and fears of the harm it could do. One couple had a disastrous history. Poor, desperate, with three badly damaged children vasectomy was realistic: it was clear to a sensitive doctor that this and their love-life represented a kind of joint clinging by the finger-nails to such happiness as they could salvage. She was aware that the guilt and shame and misery might in other circumstances profit from airing. Yet the pain was too much and too near the surface, and she intuitively respected their pitiful defences. They did well. But in another, the transvestite husband seemed to be looking to vasectomy as a kind of self-castrating punishment for his shameful secret. Vasectomy was not recommended and he admitted the request was a cry for help. He was referred for psychotherapy.

At a less serious level, several wives said they hoped it might 'cool their man down'. Challenged by her doctor as to whether she really hoped for this, one girl burst out laughing and replied that she guessed she was only boasting about him really!

We were interested to meet a number of young, childless, sometimes not even yet married or sexually committed requesters, whom I came to think of as the 'escapers'. We were all anxious about these. We found at follow-up that at least one was no longer 'with' the same member of the commune that he had brought to the session. One doctor had a thank-you letter from one such couple from a tent on the slopes of Mount Kenya. Another young pair were delighted. They had been saving up since their engagement for this. She preferred horses; he was a lone long-distance yachtsman. They went off vasectomized and penniless to Australia, holding hands and quite uncomprehending of my anxieties! Such couples would present plausible and idealistic notions about the population explosion and that the world is no place to bring children into unless you are really crazy about them. This was seductive, endearing even, but I had my own reservations about it, partly because of one young man who talked this way and who to no surprise of mine came for, and had, though not from me, a vasectomy. His first marriage had failed, his wife taking his one beloved son. I knew of old that in his own childhood the world had seemed so hostile that to risk again having — and perhaps losing — a child whom he might come to love was too difficult for him. But he maintained his 'idealism' to the last and had his vasectomy despite the youth of his second wife. I feared she might one day come to regret having no babies of her own, and I felt sad that I had failed to help him understand his self-destructiveness.

Finally we had a box on our form for 'overstretched motherhood', an idea which was revealed often and made sense of a number of requests in which the capacity for loving mothering had come to a halt. What was interesting was how this varied in actual quantity. Not all had three or four children under five. We met it sometimes in mothers of only one, or one and a termination. And 'fatherhood overstretched' was worthy of note too, as well as fear of fatherhood, again with a great variation in the number of children they had actually fathered.

As usual in such studies we gained a few new insights into the practice of medicine. We saw in this context, of course, always couples, so that we could perceive the marital interaction. But it was sometimes difficult to be sure what one partner really felt in the presence of the other, and we would take the opportunity of a quick private word with each during the physical examination. We found it important to examine both, for vasectomy may be foolish for a man whose wife may shortly need a hysterectomy for, say, fibroids, and one serious tumour of the testicle was discovered at routine examination of an apparently healthy man. The doctors found themselves variously uneasy in a situation where patients sought not help but a yes or no 'rubber stamp' to their own prescription for vasectomy. Some of our patients were none too keen to talk about it and resented having to justify, as they felt, a rational personal decision. Yet we sense that some of these, who refused to entertain any doubt, were the very people who needed encouragement to think twice. We acquired some sensitivity as to when to press our suspicions of unconscious ambivalence and when to leave well alone, recognizing that ultimately it was the patients' decision. We could only hope to help them make a more aware and informed one.

By the end of this study we had come to believe that one should never make permanent decisions in a crisis, and although vasectomy may sometimes be reversed, it must be regarded as permanent in case it cannot. After terminations, deaths of parents or illnesses of children, infidelities or some crisis real or imagined about the wife's pill-taking, we noticed that vasectomy was sometimes rushed to in panic, and was often unwise. Finally we proposed critieria for a good outcome. They were that the couple should reveal a good mutual relationship and confident sex-life. They needed to be sure that the decision was mutual and that there was no serious tension about who was persuading whom. We found it important that if sexual or marital difficulty did exist, this should be faced and examined before the operation and, above all, that their hopes of what the operation could achieve should be realistic. They should expect no miracle cures for other troubles from it, but know that it can provide a sperm-free ejaculation — and only that.

Now with AIDS we hope to encourage the use of condoms for safer sex, in a generation which has come largely to accept that women take the contraceptive responsibility; that for the man to 'have to' is somehow unmanly. It is hard for many to imagine that either partner might *prefer* this 'less spontaneous method'; that donning the sheath and inserting a pessary might become for the confident part of the anticipatory fun. Yet in World War II and the immediate postwar years, young men, who might have fled should we take them up on it, would let their 'packets of three' fall accidentally-on-purpose from their wallets when paying for the drinks to show what macho lads they were. Older married men too saw their use as manly towards their ladies — many even called them "protectives".

For the young whom we most wish to convince, whose tough image among their peers is paramount, 'show you care' may be the last message to appeal. 'Real men use condoms', with studded leather and a powerful bike, may well be a more effective advertisement.

11

Parenting and sexual feelings

The burden of motherhood
Motherhood and a father's response
Vaginal phantasy in pregnancy
Fear of being damaged
Birth trauma causing impotence

The joys 'Some women will put up with sex for the delights of
of sex motherhood, or having babies . . . ' is the first half of
and a truism which I suggested earlier was often true. It would,
parent- I suspect, raise few eyebrows, nor would the corollary,
hood 'Some men will put up with fatherhood and babies for
the delights of having sex.' That the other halves of
these statements are also often true, that there are women
who will put up with motherhood for the joys of sex
and some men who will put up with sex for the joys of
fatherhood may be less easy to understand. Yet many
of either sex have problems with their previously confident
sexuality when the matter of fertility and parenting has to
be faced.

Tessa: the   As the prospect of becoming parents arises, our view of
burden of our parents' sexuality may again be an important factor. Like
mother- Zoe's (Chapter 9) Tessa's mother was a remarkable woman
hood whom everyone admired, Tessa most of all. When her
husband, Tessa's father, died in an air accident in the distant
country in which he worked as an engineer, she had at once
returned to the nursing training she had completed but
never used before her marriage. She took a refresher course
in intensive care and became first a relief theatre staff nurse,
then a full-time sister. Later, she also became a magistrate.
Tessa had been about 11 when her father died. There had
been no overt mourning: she had never seen her mother
weep. Nor, then, did she and her elder sister and younger

brother weep, except sometimes secretly under the sheets. And anyway, Tessa told me, he had been away a lot. As her mother used to explain to their friends, the children had hardly known him and she would manage to make up for his absence. No, certainly she would never marry again until the children were off her hands. Her responsibility to them must come first.

Tessa too acquired a stiff upper lip. She worked hard to justify her mother's efforts on her behalf, gaining a university degree and a brave and praiseworthy independence. The loss of her father at a vulnerable age, and her mother's thereafter asexual model, did not affect Tessa's ability to enjoy a thoroughly confident love-life with the three men she had loved seriously, when I met her, at the age of 35. It is interesting, though, that the first was to become a geologist with an oil company and the second was a RAF pilot. Even if she was unconsciously seeking in them echoes of her lost father, she did not dare actually to settle for either of them — the one bound for faraway deserts, the other facing the hazards of supersonic flight. Instead she married a fellow school-teacher who had done all his travelling before he met her. A safe choice for one with her experience perhaps, but he was also an athlete and a fine sensitive lover. They were extremely happy and their love-life was all she could have wished for — until their first baby arrived. From the first day home, when she had 'really been looking forward to making love again, prickly stitches and all . . . I felt I couldn't wait to feel him inside me', Tessa found herself 'suddenly as cold as ice — pretending . . . not hurting, pretending'.

Now Tessa and her husband Tim had puzzled about this together and had themselves come up with the explanation, which seemed quite possible to me also, that in becoming a mother, Tessa had been somehow reminded of how mothers may have to cope alone, perhaps finding it difficult to trust their man-trusting feelings in sex. Indeed, they had wondered about this from the start, and had waited until both felt confident that nothing could harm their relationship before trying for this much-wanted baby son. Tim was, Tessa said, 'marvellous with children'. He had been present and supportive at the birth and had always taken pleasure in doing his share of chores and nappy-changing and getting up in the night. So we found ourselves agreeing that Tessa's devastatingly sudden frigidity, and the near-depression which had followed, must have a different explanation. And yet she was sure, and it made sense to me, that it was 'becoming a mother' that was the trouble. She had even been aware once or twice, as yet again Tim came to her and yet again she found her thoughts wandering to the baby, that it was a sense of burdensome responsibility, quite irrational, that came into her head, 'or perhaps into my vagina, which is worse', and switched her off.

To shorten rather a long story, we found ourselves needing to review Tessa's view of motherhood, how very painful it was, for her genuine admiration for her mother was important to Tessa and cherished by her. But this was not, of course, the whole story. Tessa began to recall sadness, resentment even, that in her brave attempts to provide for her children, her mother was not around very much herself. We explored the aspects of Tessa and her siblings that must have longed to weep, to demand some of the attention that, Tessa could now admit, they felt all had to go to 'her bloody patients'. That the self-sacrifice was to be admired was undeniable. But to wish to be otherwise — greedy, un-brave, mourning or irresponsible — was not merely less good but quite unthinkable in the family value system. This made the burdens of motherhood the greater, ironically, for Tessa, since none of it had been fully conscious.

Her guilt at recognizing that she had some dissatisfactions with this perfect mother was awful for Tessa, but it was a relief, too, for her to see that, as a child, she had been reasonably entitled to them. We could then see that despite the surface model of perfection in mothering, to which it was part of Tessa's inner burden to aspire, her own experience of being mothered had really been quite shaky. Her busy mother, even when available, had tended to overlook her children's natural neediness and 'weaknesses' in favour of offering a model of courage and independence and 'do it yourself'. These perceptions were eventually enough to free Tessa to enjoy her sex-life with Tim to the full again — for herself. After their next baby, a daughter, was born, the problem did not recur.

Not many patients whose view of motherhood is confused have such clear-cut explanations as we found for Tessa. Whatever our actual experience of mothering has been, however our actual mothers are able to get across to us intentionally or unintentionally that loving mothering and remaining a sexual individual can exist side by side within us, we must be aware yet again that the individual child's capacity to absorb this with comfort varies with the child. In therapy, all we have to work with is the viewpoint and perception of the 'child' — now themselves a mother or a father. We have heard many examples in other contexts of the fact that some 'children' need to see their parents as asexual, and hence to believe that as parents themselves, they must be asexual too. But how often it happens that a mother tries hard, only to find that her child feels that she is sending confusing messages. Tessa's mother was there as much as she could be, and undoubtedly doing her best. Indeed, if we could fault her efforts, it was perhaps for needing to give an image of perfectionist, 'professional' mothering with the sense of burden that implied for a lively developing Tessa.

I meet those for whom, more obviously, Mother was seen as a tart, a tramp, with many men of her own and keeping them for herself. Or conversely, for another kind of 'virtuous' daughter, muddling through her adolescent impressions of manhood as represented by Father, the perception is that Mother keeps her men, and Father especially, to herself. Sexual though Mother may be, it is for her alone and daughter must remain excluded. This is the other side of the 'Electra' dilemma. The fact that love for Father is not only prohibited, but implies treacherous rivalry and infidelity towards Mother, may be revived when memories of mothers and fathers are revived by becoming mothers and fathers ourselves. And then there are mothers who have seemed to their young to have been poor models of how it is done, not by hiding their own needs like Tessa's, but by being incompetent, or 'for ever', as one said, 'down the pub'.

Those mothers who just seem too busy to give their children the feeling of enough time for personal individual interest come in many perceived forms. *Working mothers* Working mothers must certainly accept these risks, when they have and enjoy children. My own eldest son, as we talked of what chaotic shambles their childhood must have seemed, was generous enough to tell me, 'Well, I suppose we learned something about surviving in a community!' And for myself — and I have heard many doing-their-best mothers say the same —

I often felt the more neglectful when I was there with them, at their disposal, merely by longing to relax with a cup of coffee and the crossword puzzle for ten minute's peace; ten minutes to myself, not having to listen to the continuous prattle, which I truly did love so very well . . . for what felt like 23¾ hours of the day! My youngest son, in response to his schoolteacher's request for an essay about his mother, produced the most succinct account of the problems of working women that I have heard. Then aged about seven, he wrote:

> My mother is a doctor.
> She cleans the house.
> She has got grey hairs.

Yet others I have heard have been brought up by a nanny or an au-pair, or reared in foster homes or even children's homes among a crowd. My anger sometimes rises up at the negligence of a mother who could and should have been there and just could not be bothered. Quite often, in fact, such children learn to cope from the start, at no very obvious cost emotionally. They have found their substitutes, or learned to manage with the shortcomings they have in mothering terms, with no apparent pathology, except perhaps a tendency to go off sex to varying degrees after becoming parents themselves. Some, particularly men, often idealize their apparently neglectful mothers. Perhaps the alternative, that is to take on board their early pain and rage towards her, would be too difficult. In emotional matters we do meet so many examples of that latter-day beatitude which goes, 'Blessed are they who expect nothing; for they shall not be disappointed.'

The thera- In psychosexual work, with only a few sessions at our
peutic disposal, we must value what short-cuts there are (bearing
approach in mind always that one man's short-cut is often another's blind alley). A colleague who sees patients in the obstetric and gynaecological department of a university medical school, often meets post-partum sexual difficulty and post-partum depression, which can, in my experience, be a deeper version from very similar roots. She has made them a particular interest and study [11] and has come independently to a very similar concept as I have with regard to these

secondary sexual problems and their treatment. I have called it 'resonating'; she calls it, more descriptively, 'the echo' which I will explain. Let us put aside for a moment the old concept of trauma and notice that in growing from infancy to parenthood we all have experiences, good, bad and indifferent, memorable or not.

In the early days of psychosexual study the pioneers became very, what we now regard as a joke, 'psychotherapeutic', meaning nothing of the kind! So does almost every new doctor who enters training. By this I mean taking long, tedious, 'psychological' histories about every member of the family into the third and fourth generation and which paternal great-grandmother had been frightened of spiders. But Tom Main would cut through this impatiently, as it seemed to us then, and say, 'Look. Everyone in the world was born and grew up and most of them went to school and liked some people and disliked others and so on and so on. And this made of them the person you have before you for living examination today. With only one clinical lifetime to work in, it is the things *they* find themselves saying to *you*, remembering verbally and non-verbally, that are relevant now. Put your notes away, and just tell us what *you* remember: *your* living impressions.' From this acquired selectivity, our work progressed so that we came to see that if we asked too many questions or took too detailed a history, all we had, as he put it, were 'answers', whereas by waiting and listening, we heard that which the patient, not always fully consciously, selected from their history as emotionally important to the matter in hand.

I had this technical distinction brought home to me forcibly by my own analyst. I, Like Zillah, was rabbitting on with all kinds of clever theoretical ideas about my own 'psychology'. After a while he dryly remarked, quite uninterested in all my complex 'self-analytic' bright ideas, 'Well, I notice you're determined to be your own therapist again today.' How much more enlightening that was about my need for 'do-it-yourself', for proud and arrogant, as I saw it ('omnipotent', he called it), independence. How common is this syndrome among us 'independent' women, invaluable as far as the creative part of our lives is concerned

Depen-
dence
diffi-
culties

but a heavy burden in terms of the child within. This sense that we have to cope unaided; that the troubles of the world are our responsibility; often develops at an age before we could possibly be expected, except by our inner selves, to understand or to cope. Tom Main suggests that even the development of high intelligence may be an early-acquired defensive process for some against the terrors inspired by such feelings. I wonder. It is certainly true that a high IQ and difficulties with 'dependence' very often go hand-in-hand for the sort of women, and men, who have problems of this kind.

We have of course also to be on the alert for what patients choose not to remember. Michael Balint drew attention to Sherlock Holmes' interesting clue of the dog which did *not* bark in the night. Tessa's omission of the slightest hint of dissatisfaction about her mother was in this category, and so was Zillah's inability to trust me to be 'right' about any of those 'psychological' matters for which she was paying good money, she declared, to be 'helped by an expert.'

To return to the idea of the 'echo'; working thus open-mindedly, we find that brief flashes of associated memory do arise from many a patient, as did Sid's recollection (Chapter 9) of overhearing his parents' lovemaking. Such a recollection may be less dramatic, but often we may hear clues as to why a certain set of circumstances in current adult life echoes or resonates with earlier incidents which have been long forgotten, but which have a comparable emotional content to those events which give problems and distress today. Thus a contemporary event which in itself should be rationally comprehensible resonates with a comparable set of emotional circumstances at an age when the circumstances and the emotional reaction to them were not fully comprehensible. They can then take on the irrational or even nightmare quality (since they are not remembered with conscious logic) which produces sexual difficulty or some other psychosomatic symptom in adult life.

Tony: sexual difficulty with 'mothers'   I only met Tony once, but I knew his wife Thelma well, as she came annually for her routine Pap smear investigation and general check-up since their daughter was born some 12 years ago. Tony's enthusiasm for lovemaking had declined rapidly, Thelma told me, after the birth of their first baby, a son, and since the arrival of the second, a girl, he had virtually never approached her again. When he had, as between the two babies, his erection was slow to arise despite the tricks of encouragement she had always been able to offer him successfully before the child was born. By now, if she so much as rested her arm across him in sleep, he would push her away.

Thelma had been confused and desperately hurt by this in the early days — had tried 'everything'. That 'everything' had included having a full vaginal repair, though she had had no severe symptoms of her own, in the belief that a crass and casual remark of Tony's, at a moment of his own failure and humiliation, that she was a 'stretched old bag' since the births, might literally be true, and that surgical tightening up might help him feel differently about her. This helped not at all, for clearly it was Tony's inner vision of her, now a mother, which was represented in that cruel remark about her anatomy.

Only having seen Tony once, I cannot elaborate on his difficulty with any accuracy but the story he gave me was very like others I have heard. In essence, he simply could not find it possible to be sexually excited by someone who had become a mother. From what Thelma told me, it seemed that his problem had the classic Oedipal roots of prohibitions on sexuality towards mother figures. He told me himself that he had been quite a confident lover, not only in the early years of their marriage but with other younger girls (and boys) before and since. The homosexuality was offered in a shame-faced, throw-away fashion by a man who, as a successful stockbroker, had merely come obediently to please his wife, to be confronted by yet another daunting mother figure in me. It did not, however, have the sound of more than adolescent experimentation. He and Thelma had been lively and eager lovers, usually on her initiative, before she had become a mother. His own mother, according to Thelma, was a 'ghastly woman', but I have no way of verifying that!

I had many opportunities over the years to try with Thelma to see whether she had problems of her own or whether she had herself changed in some way with motherhood. We had never come up with anything. I found only the hurt, as I checked the diaphragm she keeps 'just in case', as she said wryly, 'for you never know your luck'. We discussed whether she might find a lover. Until now she has not wanted to. It would be difficult in her social circle. Her own work is to help in her husband's office; they do not often meet unattached friends, and she is not the kind to set off on the hunt. What excuse, she says, could she make to her children, her friends? She is now, 12 years on, angry as well as hurt enough to say that should some Prince Charming now appear, she would let her husband know, for reasons of practical planning as much as to punish him.

It is simply a great pity that a loving and, from choice, faithful woman has to manage without a whole chunk of her personality, which was once a joy to them both. Tony's mother, according to Thelma, was a successful actress: narcissistic, possessive of Tony still, but in a characteristic way. Apparently she even now 'shows him off . . . waving him like a flag' or, Thelma feels, 'as though he is a pet puppy, for people to admire and be amused by, not as a man, but as a production of hers'. Yet he is expected to drop everything when she needs him — as an escort, or to sort out her endless financial incompetencies. In one of her understandably less charitable moods (which only I am privileged to share, for Thelma has now achieved an amicable *modus vivendi* at home), she told me that Tony's mother always had a 'tame man' on her arm, and that they get younger and younger — 'hairdressers, dancing teachers, golf professionals'. Even as I write, I notice a dog not barking. Did Tony ever have a father? No strong model, it seems, of how to cope with such 'mothers' real or symbolic, as in Thelma or me. None remembered at least, none reported to me.

Could Thelma have foreseen this, knowing his mother as she did? We may with hindsight wonder whether she might have been forewarned. Yet Tony's feelings toward this overpowering woman seemed well in hand and conscious until the specifically sexual difficulty with 'mothers' emerged, when Thelma herself became a mother.

Terry: vaginal phantasy in pregnancy   I knew another with a very similar story who perhaps might have been forewarned, for her second husband did show clearly, again with hindsight, that his feelings toward his also eccentric mother were perhaps even more disturbed. Tara however had her own reasons for extra caution this time around, and was thus, it seemed, blind to the warning signs as Terry dithered about her wish for a child. He made excuses, changed his mind even after the pregnancy, by then 'planned', was achieved. Tara, now a successful designer in her own right, had married very young, in hero-worship, a young musician who turned out to be more deeply into hard drugs than she had realized. Thus, after an early divorce, she was all too anxious to get it right next time, to find someone, as she felt Terry to be, 'safer', more like her reliable, devoted father and brothers. She was not aware, in their confident early days together, that there might be problems developing in his 'dog-like devotion' (her words) to this 'old cow' of a demanding mother; that he had reached 40 without serious sexual commitment, and that his previous girlfriends had been 'a series of lighthearted youngsters'. She saw this only as proof that he had been, as she had, 'waiting for the right one to come along'. They had indeed loved well and much, until her pregnancy threw him into what sounded like a really severe disturbance. He was unable to touch her, feeling that her vagina had acquired 'teeth', and that if these did not bite his penis and testicles off, those of the baby inside her surely would.

I hope Terry found help. I had only Tara's confusion and horror to work with, which was enough, but in this instance it did sound as though his was the primary problem. I knew another man who was only ever fully potent with prostitutes. Religious and hence full of self-disgust about this, he found himself totally repelled by his loved and kindly wife once she was delivered of their baby. He was fairly clear in his own mind that his wife had become identified then with his idealized and asexual — in his vision — mother, who had recently died, and that he had put his wife upon a pedestal which made sexual 'use of her' (his words) unthinkable. We reached the stage when he could confess something of the phantasy which made sex with prostitutes 'easier', to do, vaguely, with soiling them in some ill-defined but 'disgracefully' pleasurable and lavatorial way. I hoped I had helped him feel easier about this but evidently not; he did not return. I suspect that facing such thoughts in himself, particularly in the company of such another mother figure as I, however accepting I tried to be, was just too shameful for him.

It seems that, unusually, I have in this chapter started with the difficult ideas first. It is not often, of course, that such deep-seated pathology is involved in the very common secondary losses of sexual confidence after childbirth or conception. Only when we find simple explanatory reassurance insufficient do we need, by listening for echoes, to explore why a particular individual is so vulnerable to a particular set of circumstances as to have lost touch with what used to be a confident and untroubled sexual life. It is, for example, almost universal for first-time mothers to be a bit anxious on arriving home to cope with this dependent, burping and squalling bundle alone. All our ante-natal classes and books fade in the face of sheer panic inspired by the terrifying sense of responsibility for another life. In this situation it is almost inevitable that the libido available for sexual love is diverted somewhat, however supportive the man may be. It is further almost universal and inevitable that the young husband, newly a father and hoping and trying to share the rejoicing and the burdens, feels a little displaced. Those women with real reasons to doubt their capacity for mothering, and those men with real reason for jealousy of past rivals and young intruders, may find it less easy to cope, to be sexually patient and to retain the confidence that, given time, their passion may revive.

Problems   I touched upon the fear of being damaged in Terry. Much
after   more common is the fear for the man of causing damage
childbirth to his pregnant or recently delivered wife or to the baby within her, and for the woman of sustaining damage to herself or her baby. Naturally those who threaten to miscarry, and are advised to refrain from vigorous intercourse for the first three months, may not find it so easy to resume their sexual relationship. If the birth proved difficult, or stitches and bruising cause pain at the first attempts at intercourse after the birth clearly, that in itself, takes a little time to overcome.

When people mention these anxieties to their obstetrician at post-natal examination, even if they are told with kindness and accuracy that everything is perfectly healed, it is surprising how often they fail to be reassured. Many who have been dismayed to find intercourse difficult tend to attribute it to having changed in some physical way, like Tessa with Tony's 'stretched old bag' idea, and then find the reason 'down there'. They notice, for example, the slight asymmetry caused by a perfectly well-healed episiotomy scar, or the bubbly vaginal tissue now visible within which they had not noticed before. They then fearfully imagine lumps, or worry about the naturally increased discharge, and phantasize serious changes and damage. If they are allowed to elaborate on the precise nature of their anxiety, however irrational, true reassurance can follow with physical examination and explanation. Without such elaboration it cannot. The fear being complicated by phantasy or mis-understanding, no gynaecologist can be expected to detect the cause. This can make matters worse, for the patient may develop the further fear that the doctor must have missed it, and is therefore then not to be trusted. It is then but a short step for the frightened person to imagine it must be something even worse or beyond repair.

Fears of physical damage are by no means the only source of difficulty after childbirth. I have met many who have found it hard to recapture sexual pleasure, or even to consummate at all after birth, for whom their sense of privacy has been lost. Those who have needed surgical induction of labour, or stitching after a tear or episiotomy, often find being 'slung up' in stirrups, a practice now less frequently employed, invades privacy and causes feelings of helplessness. One mother felt like 'a beetle on its back' and said that it caused a sense that 'that part of me which used to be just for loving, could never feel mine in the same way again.' Several have attributed this feeling of invasion and exposure to the presence of student midwives or doctors, as though, one said, 'I was a floor show. If only just one of them had seemed to be looking at me and not simply at my rear end'. Yet in the second stage of labour, when most exposed, it is rare to feel this invaded sense, however many people are around. The sheer absorption in the overwhelming physical process makes mothers oblivious. It seems that, for some, those necessary obstetric processes which require exposure 'in cold blood' inter-fere with their subsequent joy in a part of them which was privately theirs before, as were the feelings of desire associated with it. This is a different emotional mechanism from that which makes the vagina and its desires then seem to belong to the baby, to the maternal self.

The sense of failure which a difficult birth or a caesarian can cause for someone who has had high hopes to 'do it well' may also lead to secondary sexual difficulty until the emotional process is satisfactorily explored. Since women have responded to the idea of controlling their own labour in the 1940s there may be a backlash effect for some who had not been prepared for the fact that contractions can be painful, and expected that the right breathing and practice would not only help but eliminate pain altogether. Many found that at the first really cracking 'pain' — what else should we call it? — they panicked, thinking something had gone wrong. If this panic went unrecognized — as it so often can be in a busy maternity unit, especially for women who are trying to be brave and 'sensible' — and the woman was told she 'wasn't doing anything much yet . . . just breathe away, dear', this became a true crisis of confidence. 'I thought', said one who had been determined to do it naturally and well, 'if this is "nothing much" I'm not going to make it.' I propose, though I can never prove it, that it may be panic which leads to some really difficult forceps deliveries, stemming from the inability from that moment on to relax as had been practised.

Today we have a number of excellent and sane approaches to natural childbirth, as well as a few that are less sound. Again, I see many who might have done better, have been less shocked by the natural hazards and discomforts of any first birth, had they not been encouraged to have unrealistic expectations, or to set such store on 'doing it themselves'. Of course, I do not subscribe to the view that regards pregnancy and birth as a disease and I do subscribe to the view which allows parents the maximum possible choice of management. Whose body is it after all?

But I do meet many for whom their own insistence and their difficulty in trusting their experienced obstetric advisers can lead to problems. This is more prevalent, I find, among that generation who have decided to wait for their babies until 30-ish or more. Naturally, these brave new women want to show the same good planning in giving birth as they have in their careers and the management of their lives. Admirably, they read the books, attend the classes; less wisely, they decide they will never agree to certain obstetric interventions, including induction, episiotomy or analgesia.

Some suspect that these methods are designed for the convenience of the labour ward staff. If it were true it would be unprofessional, but it has not been my experience. This resistance to obstetric intervention is not so excellent if such procedures are really necessary to the health of the mother or to the life of the baby.

It is sad that the term 'natural' — particularly in relation to childbirth as well as to diet and 'medicines' in general — has become a commercial sales pitch. Babies have, albeit rarely, drowned during water births. Truly 'natural' childbirth *can* mean bleeding to death in the jungle.

I met one sweet, thoughtful girl only recently who had felt just like this. She had been so desperately keen to give birth 'naturally and well' that she adamantly refused an episiotomy, seeing it, as some natural childbirth article had suggested, as an unnecessary raping intrusion. She had, for her pains, suffered quite a severe tear, only just missing the anus. She had been ill-informed. I feel somewhat anxious too about the view that epidural analgesia should be every woman's right. Certainly, if it is necessary, but it is a procedure requiring a high degree of technical skill. As an alternative to general anaesthesia for emergency procedures it was a tremendous breakthrough, but not necessarily desirable as a comfort for every normal birth.

Men as well as women can be devastated, disappointed or disturbed by events at the birth itself. I met a tough man, a man among men, who became totally impotent after bravely attending his baby's normal birth. Nick might have been forewarned by his flickers of unease at being shown the labour ward, 'all that chrome and glass and gadgetry', during the classes which he attended faithfully to support hs wife Nora. All the other men at the Rugby Club had supported their wives, but not all the men at the Rugby Club were prone to 'go queasy' at injections or at the sight of blood. Maybe, too, not all would have been quite as ashamed of such a 'weakness' as Nick, so keen to overcome something he saw as 'wet'. Thus, feeling some anxiety as to how they could cope in the labour ward, they might have dared to say, 'No thanks. You know me. I might pass out, and then what help would I be?' Not so Nick. He did his

Nick: fear of being damaged

best, nauseous throughout, holding Nora's hand, wiping her brow, rubbing her back, delirious with joy (and perhaps relieved triumph to have made it without passing out) at the birth of his hefty son. But then, tragically he experienced terrified impotence after. He could confess to me, weeping, that the labour ward had been for him 'like an abattoir, doctor'. Not surprisingly, it was the irrational terror of what 'he had caused' that made his erection flag at the mere idea of further penetration of this 'damaged', by him as he felt it, beloved wife. Fortunately the sharing of these perceptions was enough to allow him to recover his potency. Nora was by now safely back on the pill, but she wants more babies, for she, incredibly to Nick, actually enjoyed it! Who knows whether, when the time comes to try for the next, or the next is born that Nick's nightmares will be revived. 'One thing is sure,' he says, 'I'm not about to be there next time. I'll stay home and play with the young 'un.' I believe he may cope, because he could confess his terrors and share with me his 'wet weakness' without too much shame.

Norman: Norman had a vasectomy after the birth of his only son, *birth* and it was this, his wife Nesta believed, which had caused *trauma* his virtually total impotence ever since. We soon discovered *causing* that Norman had been in trouble from the moment when *terrified* the child was born with a heart defect, caused by rubella *impotence* that Nesta had caught early in her pregnancy. They had asked their family doctor whether anything should be done and he had not found it necessary to advise an injection. This was some years ago when medical knowledge was incomplete; perhaps Norman's own memory of 'thinking he had heard of "vaccination"' was flawed. Norman's feeling that he, Norman, should have insisted, or at least that he should have agreed to termination of the pregnancy, which was Nesta's, now guilt-ridden, first thought. She, they both agreed, had been none too keen to start a family yet anyway. She had had elderly relatives to care for and was only just free of them. She enjoyed her job and their thoroughly lively sex life and felt there was plenty of time to conceive. It was Norman who was keen about having babies. As an only child himself, he could not wait to have a houseful of pattering, tiny feet. So Norman's sense of full responsibility for this child was evident. No wonder he, in his guilt and dismay, rushed in panic for vasectomy, to be sure he could do no harm again. He was adamant. Refused by his family doctor, who thus emerges as not quite as negligent as they accused him of being over the rubella, Norman went straight to a private surgeon, who, according to them, 'asked no questions'. He did not, of course, have our and the family doctor's awareness that here was a man who had longed for a large family. Had he, he might have thought twice about what had caused such a frantic change of heart within two weeks of the arrival of Norman's first-born.

Twenty years on, a loving pair, devoted to although over-protective towards a lad who was apparently fit and independent enough to have got to technical college and to represent it at competitive, if not too high-powered, soccer, sought help! Norman's impotence had continued. Only when something happened to give him massive encouragement, such as his son's sporting achievements, would his sexuality revive briefly until Nesta's pre-menstrual tension, or some other minor irritation, would reawaken his sense of guilt and failure. Then his erections would fail again and he would become increasingly clinically depressed, prone to psychosomatic episodes of 'weakness' and unable to feel safe driving his car, symptoms which a battery of experts, psychiatric and medical, had failed to elucidate in his many hospital admissions over all these years.

The cost not only to Norman's marriage but to his effectiveness at work through these unconfident years is beyond measure. Financially, one might add that the cost to the National Health Service of his many months of inpatient care, of the multitude of inevitable but expensive and fruitless investigations, had also been considerable. Airing the likely source of this depressed rage and guilt and the self-castration represented in the vasectomy did help them both, for Nesta had her own sense of guilt at having fleetingly wished to 'damage' her son by abortion. Temporarily at least, Norman regained his confident sexuality. He stopped his tablets, went back to work and drove his car without fear of passing out (the worst fear there, predictably, was that he would 'go out of control and hurt someone'). With such a long and severe history we may expect Norman to be vulnerable to further pitfalls in the future. But if the importance of fatherhood to Norman's sexuality had been recognized earlier, what waste might have been avoided.

12

Abortion and ambivalence

The need to deny helplessness
The baby within
Underlying sibling rivalry
Mourning

Abortion is an emotive and contentious subject. That the *The* woman who is directly concerned, and those she loves, *woman's* should have mixed and deep feelings about it is not only *choice* inevitable but proper. That her advisers, medical and legislative, should be equally affected and even swayed by passionate prejudices of their own is less useful, but perhaps equally inevitable. Sally MacIntyre, in a taut and sensitive sociological study in Aberdeen [12], showed clearly, however, that the outcome of a request for termination of pregnancy depended significantly upon her doctor's personal and sometimes rigid views. As with many of the topics illustrated here, it is futile to discuss abortion in the abstract. Unwanted pregnancy ought not to be subject merely to an empirical procedure which any professional should be for or against, even for religious reasons, outside the context of the individual human experience. It is no accident that even in medical circles we tend to use the emotive term 'abortion' to imply a deliberate act, 'miscar-riage' to imply an accident. Students are taught that, technically, the two terms are interchangeable. Value judgements are imposed in the language used.

Many believe that moral philosophy and ethics are the fundamental considerations for a worried woman and her doctor in this dilemma. I shall not argue with them here. Studies have been made, however, of the difficulties for the woman herself, and for her adviser, in what is by definition a panic situation if either is not fully conscious of the conflicting feelings within them [13, 14]. For those of us who must professionally advise or legislate it seems to me that to know that we do not and cannot know the perfect answer is as useful a starting-point as any when it comes to enabling the individual in trouble to make as conscious and constructive a decision as possible. Their situation is confused and confusing; always, at least minimally, ambivalent and potentially guilt-ridden, even for those who would wish to regard termination on demand as their inalienable right, and as of no more moral or emotional significance than having a tooth out.

Even some of these may not find it so easy unless offered an opportunity, before the decision is made, to face the inner flicker which would decide otherwise. These considerations must always, I believe, be weighed against the medical and social advantages of 'the sooner the better'. It takes no longer to say: 'this can be arranged if you are sure it is what you need. Now let us think for a moment about any regrets you may have later', than to wrangle defensively over right and wrong. In my experience, sexual and other emotional difficulties are more likely to arise after terminations if these mixed feelings have not been aired beforehand. Once the deed is done the motivation to rethink is more difficult, since there is no way back. The need to deny doubts increases. It is my personal belief that ultimately only the woman can decide whether the risk to her emotional or physical health and that of those around her will be more damaged by termination or by continuance. But as a clinician I feel responsible for ensuring that her choice is based on considerations which are as fully and consciously informed as possible.

Vicky: the need to deny helplessness   The mutual friend who suggested to Vicky that she visit me told me, 'You'll find her one tough cookie.' It took a while to get us together as one appointment after another was postponed by Vicky's efficient secretary, while Vicky herself had to leave unexpectedly on business trips to Birmingham or Bremen or Boston, Mass. At 31, Vicky had made a considerable success of her agency in the tough, competitive world of advertising. Some capacity for ruthlessness must, she herself believed, have been required, but it later became clear that her ruthlessness was above all directed towards herself. Nevertheless, when I at last met Vicky I could identify easily with the doctor who had originally, eight years ago, acceded to her demand for termination without question. Vicky, elegant and clever, gave the impression of being totally in command of herself and her arguments. She would, I can imagine, have given no hint of uncertainties.

At that time Vicky was already living committedly with the same man as now. Their love-life had been good. He too was successful, in a parallel world to hers. Both were ambitious, and even then they were far from the breadline. Why had they given no consideration whatever to parenthood, with or without marriage? Perhaps Vicky simply knew what she was about and made a legitimate choice. Many do, and why should they not? Equally though, with hindsight, perhaps she made it difficult for her previous doctor to see or consider that she had any doubts, because it was so difficult for her to have insight into any such vulnerable confusion within herself, let alone to show it. This is speculation. Certainly, when I met Vicky, she was apparently denying any such doubts, but beneath the tough image, as we talked about why she should need quite such a hard shell in her personal life too, it was clear that the alternatives were difficult for Vicky. While consciously and fruitfully making the most of her efficiency and intellect and business sense at work, less consciously she had deeper terrors of vulnerability and dependency in private life should she let this defensive guard down. By now she could confess the problem which had brought her to me: she had never fully enjoyed intercourse since their termination. She wept a little, then brusquely apologized, as though her tears were shameful to her. The fact of her friend having to do her help-seeking for her, her many postponements of our meeting for business reasons, legitimate though they were, began to take on a different light. Her difficulty was in revealing need and in giving her wish for better loving a high priority.

We could see together that there was some parallel between this and her difficulty in admitting or giving high priority to the unconscious part of her which might have wanted the baby, or in seeking her man's support or opinion (she had not consulted him), or even perhaps in acknowledging the possibility of doubt. She might thus have allowed her previous doctor too some chance to 'take care of her' if she had wished, rather than meekly signing the form without question. We may not criticize the doctor or Vicky. This was her personality and she was the same with everyone and with me, until we could identify this 'dog that did not bark in the night' and acknowledge her great need to deny any inner vulnerabilities.

With Vicky it emerged that it was the 'self-trusting' part of her which seemed to get into difficulty after the termination, with no other outwardly ill-effects than the inability to 'trust' subsequently her own instincts in bed; to trust her own desires for abandonment and any feeling of dependence that she had towards her perfectly stable and trustworthy lover. She was reminded during our conversations of being left alone in the dark as a child to cry. After this visit, her second, she actually offered to postpone a business meeting in order to come again soon. We could share the idea that to admit to her need for help and to trust me was in itself an important step for her. When she returned she reported that her love-life had improved. She had been able to weep on her man's shoulder about the past, and they were thinking that marriage and a baby need not necessarily interfere with her job at this stage, though they had not yet decided whether they wanted either. He, we may not be surprised to hear — though it surprised Vicky — confessed he had been very hurt by the ending of 'their child', even more so because she had been unable to trust him with the option to support her or even to voice his opinion.

Our experience of so many like Vicky who need to deny any helplessness led us to think about some requests for termination in terms of the patient's vision of 'the baby within herself'. Often it seems such women are not only wishing to get rid of an unwanted or inconvenient pregnancy, as their moral critics believe, and as I believe is their right if they are sure, but for some inner reason need unconsciously also to 'get rid of' whatever bit of themselves is seen as babyish, and thus unacceptable. For Vicky the vivid image of helpless childishness left unsupported, alone crying in the dark, made sense to me at least, and did to her, as but one good reason to feel that it is necessary to cope emotionally unaided. To be reminded by an actual baby within of the other symbolic 'baby' within Vicky — that vulnerable bit of herself — led, it seems, to a revival of the associated symbolic defence. Such a 'baby' is too helpless, too needy. Such disturbing, needy feelings must be annihilated. Vicky had almost succeeded in killing off, at least from her own and others' overt awareness, that 'baby' bit of her own persona. That in so doing she had actually 'killed' a potential baby may or may not give her pain for the future.

I have met many who have had terminations for good *Inner* reasons but who never quite recapture their early sexual or *guilt* emotional confidence until they have conceived and continued a successful pregnancy. It is not always so simple. Some find it difficult to conceive again, although investigations reveal no physical harm done by the earlier operation. Without exploring their inner guilt and ambivalence, sexual pleasure and/or conception are difficult. Once these feelings are explored, I have known several such women conceive and carry a baby to term without further problems. Yet others may conceive but carry a great deal of anxiety over the inner 'baby destroying' aspect of them. They may have difficult births or severe anxiety about caring for their baby once born, as though they feel inadequate, even dangerous, towards the now much wanted child. It is as though the outside world has not punished them and they must therefore punish themselves.

The precise view of the 'baby' element in us will, of course, mean different things to each of us, and those for whom babyishness holds no terrors or who have long since come to comfortable terms with their own 'babyishness', will not be vulnerable to difficulties of this nature. I am impressed at how often, in discussing sexual or emotional problems of any kind, a patient, male or female, will use the word 'childish' about some aspect of their deeper feelings — and use it with contempt. If one offers instead the expression 'childlike', which sounds so much less critical, more attractive, the conversation can take a very different turn, and one can begin to suggest that such people may be their own worst critics in this respect.

Another twist to this 'baby inside ourselves' phenomenon *Violet:* which I meet often is, as it were, the other side of the coin. *the baby* Some who become pregnant accidentally and unwisely, *within* reveal that they have apparently unconsciously sought to *find* the baby within themselves in this way. Violet, the middle child of a busy family, became pregnant at 15. Her parents, schoolteachers and family doctor swept her off for termination, her feet hardly touching the ground — and perhaps wisely for, though a lively and intelligent girl with the future before her, she was 'in no way mature enough to cope unaided with a real live baby', as she put it. Her opinion was not sought and she felt very strongly later that though they were 'of course quite right', it was the public disgrace that they were concerned about. The conception had been with a mere friend: 'Everyone was doing it.' she said, 'or rather', for she was a perceptive girl, 'so they said'. She was shattered by the abortion and did not have intercourse again for a while, but at 17 she met a boy at a disco whom she did 'fancy a lot'. Despite knowing about contraception by then, she conceived again. By this time it was clear to me that far from being irresponsible, and 'boy mad', Violet found no mature enjoyment in her own emerging sexuality; indeed it was by now shame-ridden. Her need to become pregnant was some kind of attention-seeking — a message to her parents, perhaps. We were able to explore these feelings a bit, before her second termination was arranged and contraception advised, in case she wanted to make love again positively for herself. When I last saw her she was sitting A-levels with a conditional offer of a university place. She was wondering, should she achieve adequate grades whether she might be able to change her course to psychology . . .

Under-   The useful work with Violet was, I believe, about allowing
lying   her to get in touch with her bitter but unaware envy of the
sibling attention her younger siblings received. This emerged
rivalry through exploration of her formerly unconscious wish for 'a baby of her own' and thus for the 'baby' in herself that was the part of her that she felt had been loved and lovable in them, and in her before they came. It did not seem necessary then, though it may be one day when she seriously considers motherhood, to explore the further rivalry with her own mother. She was able to say, however, that when the time came she would look after her own babies 'better', and that it was something to do with that which must have led her unwittingly to 'prove something' by becoming pregnant. We could wryly agree together that in so far as she needed this 'baby-wishing' part of her to be noticed, at the same time feeling that she was barely entitled to it and deserved punishment for it, that she had

certainly achieved her aim! There had been no shortage of volunteers rallying round to fuss her protectively, and in the doing, ironically, to reinforce the idea that it must be hidden, stopped forthwith, aborted in more ways than one.

Others like Violet are not so lucky in understanding their inner processes, and if any such confusion leads to repeated 'accidental' pregnancy, punitive lectures about irresponsibility will prove futile unless the inner driving force has been elicited and understood. Few people would be wilfully destructive either to their babies or to the 'babies' within themselves without reason.

I have been interested, however, to notice the recent phenomenon among that generation who have been able to use the pill from the very beginning of their sexual lives. Several have stopped taking it, or stopped using any other contraceptive method, for no logical reason that they could give me. I do not mean those for whom medical reasons, or even frightening newspaper reports, have provided rational indications for a rest. One of these women, accidentally pregnant and seeking termination in distress and amazement, said to me: 'Somehow I had taken it for granted for so long, that it seemed it could never happen to me.'

For some, then, it seems that the dissociation between sexual pleasure and fertility made possible by effective contraception in which most people rejoice, has backfired. It is forgotten that unprotected intercourse results in conception. I saw one successful career woman who become pregnant at 37 by omitting contraception at a light-hearted conference encounter which she herself described as a 'moment of diminished responsibility'. She could laugh at herself, ruefully, for she had truly never wanted children. Her long-standing relationship with a man who already had grown-up children from his long-dead first wife suited them both as it was. She could volunteer without any interpretation from me: 'It is as though I suddenly found myself wanting to prove that I could' (become pregnant), 'before it was too late.' No deep exploration was required here, but I have met others in like situations for whom the sense of rivalry with the ghost of the other wife — the 'mother' in more ways than one — can cause pain and confusion in second relationships, however loving, which are infertile whether by accident or rational choice.

Illegal There is always much controversy in Britain as to whether
abortion the Abortion Law needs modifying: whether only 'medical'
rather than 'social' reasons for termination should be legally
acceptable. I hope I have illustrated that in my opinion
emotional considerations can legitimately be deemed
'medical'. Those who today argue strongly about the evils
of abortion 'on demand', identifying with the revulsion felt
by young nurses at seeing 'babies' being sluiced away, cannot but evoke sympathy; it is always a sad and even messy
business. We may be thankful, however, that such people
no longer have to witness the earlier management of
unwanted pregnancy which a less liberal law made commonplace. As a young doctor, I was a gynaecological house
officer and later a registrar in a comfortable outer London
green-belt area, in a prosperous seaside resort and in two
southern cathedral cities. In these places I was hardly at the
core of the worst of inner city poverty and back-street abortion. Yet even there it was a nightly routine to be called to
the casualty department to one woman after another:
shocked, exsanguinated, often infected, after an incomplete
abortion. I shall never forget the rush to raise the barely
detectable blood pressure with such intravenous fluid as was
to hand; the struggle to find the collapsed vein: the clearing
of the cervix of the clots that maintained the state of shock;
my blood-stained clothes; a yawning porter swabbing the
floor. Then the chill wait to cross-match blood in a dark
laboratory, the old-fashioned centrifuge rattling, and then
later, when we dared, the evacuation in theatre — the
anaesthetist's worried face, the search for the appropriate
antibiotic. In my experience women who are so determined,
so frantic, to abort will have it done. If our laws prevent
them having it done responsibly in decent, aseptic conditions by skilled operators, they will find their own means,
be it with their own knitting needles. We may be thankful
that our reformed law has prevented much of this horror,
and I cannot seriously believe anyone would wish to return
to it. It was a high price to pay for a woman's desperation.

However rational at the time, many find after termination that until they have a healthy baby safe in their arms,
there is some extra anxiety lest 'unpunished' ere now, some
'deserved' retribution is unconsciously expected. I call this
the 'wrath of the Gods' syndrome, met too in those whose
early lives have been 'wild', sexually or otherwise; others
who feel they have 'failed to save' some loved one and

are unable to 'forgive' themselves by sexually enjoying a new relationship in widow- or usually widower-hood.

We see abortion then as an extreme example of personal dilemma. For the individual concerned, generalizations about ethics are useless. Indeed in so far as most people try to act rightly as well as sensibly, such pressures can only prove an added source of conflict. If the tension between the wish to be free of the 'problem' — posed in this instance by the 'baby' — and possible dreams or regrets about what might have been, are not faced, a promising relationship or a woman's progress towards confident adult sexuality may be aborted along with the pregnancy. While it may be harder for a woman to trust her instincts in love again if her partner leaves her or fails to support her in these decisions, some men too carry their own shame at the 'quitter' within them and then have problems with their own sense of entitlement to sexual pleasure afterwards.

Pregnancy is not the only fact of life about which people *Mourning* have to make positive decisions when their inner feelings are ambivalent. They may need to examine and mourn not only the lost babies within their bodies or within their inner selves, but for lost ideas, lost dreams, lost parts of themselves in so many ways. Further, when such decisions are not of their own making, when the might-have-been is snatched from them by outer circumstances over which they have no control, the need to mourn may be the greater. If such circumstances echo, resonate, with earlier less comprehensible pain, they may need help to understand and accept the added, less conscious nightmare quality before they can mourn freely and well and begin to recover. If guilt about negative feelings or about inadequacies or loving care exists, any natural mourning process may be prolonged into true depression.

Whether it is a person who is mourned, a dream or a part of the self, the conscious anguish of parting, of loneliness, is but one aspect, which is hard enough in itself to bear, and even harder if it echoes an earlier experience of less comprehended parting, desertion, or loneliness. Inner guilts for what might have been done give greater torment if aggravated by some inner sense of being prone to fail, that an inner something has failed earlier to keep love, or driven people to rejection. Furthermore, it may be unbearable to know consciously about the inner rage at desertion and the guilt and despair at that anger itself.

It is hard for those who are brought up to be, and indeed would wish to be, brave, civilized and rational, to be confronted by such primitive turbulent aspects of inner feelings, normal and natural though they may be in the circumstances. How many 'sensible' mothers, I wonder, have shared with me the determination to be wise and unfussed, to avoid being over-protective, when our children have seemed to be under threat or are risking actually dangerous adventures? How disturbing to find oneself feeling inside not only terrified but savage in their defence, as a tiger for her cubs! How astonishing is this awareness, how hard to calm ourselves in the face of it. Adrenalin is designed to prepare us for fight or flight in a self-preservation response to stress and fear. In modern society, among the 'well-behaved', there seems to be no place to run.

Depres-
sion and
sexual
difficulty
The relationship between sadness and depression, depression and sexual difficulty, is a subtle and complex one. Clinically it is important, for it is not, I believe, sadness alone that often causes that apathetic withdrawal which we call true depression. Often it may be the need to *suppress* rage or sadness which causes it. Psychiatrists argue about how far depression is emotionally reactive or if it is caused by chemical imbalance, but in psychosexual medicine the distinction is important. Clearly if a patient is truly clinically depressed in a general sense, in response to external events or from within themselves, they may also be sexually apathetic, and to attempt to treat the sexual difficulty without acknowledging the underlying depression is to treat the symptom rather than the illness which is futile and misguided. Surprisingly, however, by no means all depressed patients lose their sexual capacity. I have met those for whom it was the one pleasure, their only comfort and saving grace in an inner world which had become bleak and unbearable. Conversely, however, to be perpetually disappointed sexually, or to be out of touch with the lively sexual desires within, can be depressing in itself, even to the point we would call clinical depression. If the sexual problem can be resolved, and insight gained that in suppressing such a potentially life-enhancing part of the

personality, the general enjoyment of living may suffer, the depression may also be lightened.

In this context I have come to believe that we may see untroubled sexual enjoyment, and enthusiasm for it, as the finest indicators of a general sense of self-confidence and self-value. In conditions of stress or anxiety, whether originating in inner confusions or external circumstances, sexual confidence may be the first to go, the last to recover. If it seems necessary to damp down any disturbing or turbulent emotion, difficulty with uninhibited sexual feelings may also arise. If it is not possible to turn to sexual expression for simple comfort or if a partner cannot understand, sadnesses of quite another order may be expressed as sexual difficulty, which is then in danger of becoming self-perpetuating.

For some, confusions after termination may show themselves in sexual difficulty rather than in any deeper or more general unhappiness. Sometimes this is a matter of degree, but often it is because it seems to the woman or her partner to have been their unheeding sexuality which brought them this problem. I do wish to stress, however, that there are more sources of pain in the world than sex, and even though these may affect our sex-lives they will not be resolved just by the mastery of sexual techniques.

13

Losses

The need to re-learn sexual feelings
A missing uterus
Fear of menopausal madness
The dark side of homosexuality
Rage at the end of mothering
A passive response to infidelity

The pain The involuntary end to fertility, whether by hysterectomy
of loss or the menopause, is an experience which may cause much
pain, especially in women for whom mothering has been
an important part of their motivation. We may not be surprised that this sense of loss may require mourning, or that
sexual difficulties may arise if what they see as the primary
purpose of loving is coming to an end. Further, such depression or secondary frigidity may cause marital difficulty if the
reasons are not understood by a husband who is himself
coming to a stage where his own sense of achievement, of
sexual confidence and optimism, is under threat. Ageing is
especially likely to lead to problems for those who see sex
as for the young, or for whom it provides reassurance of
their value in competitive terms.

'Life begins at forty', Sophie Tucker, the film star,
sang, in a triumphant celebration of mature sexuality.
She was before her time, it would seem; certainly before
mine. We would all wish she were right, but so often
we are more likely to view that birthday as the beginning
of the end rather than the end of the beginning, and
to respond with a cry for her contemporary Mae West's
namesake, the life-jacket! A well-known therapist was
quoted as instructing all her over-40 patients to look in
the glass every morning and say to themselves: 'I am
a mature, interesting, sexy lady.' I applaud these senti-
ments and wish I had thought of the idea myself. Nevertheless, I doubt the therapist herself was yet 40 at the
time. Many find, despite our good intentions, that we

are more likely to look in the glass with dismay. This half-way stage of life is for many a watershed: a time of mixed feelings and ambivalence for men and women alike. It can be a time of sophistication and achievement, of new freedoms and challenges. Equally it may entail new self-doubts and uncertainties and future roles and expectations or disappointments and anger at missed opportunities for what might have been; the sense of 'Is it now all downhill?' and of 'Where do we go from here?'

In a world which seems to glorify youth, the 'change' tends to be seen as a change for the worse. This view needs cool, critical appraisal. The menopause is just a physiological change signalling the end of our fertility, accompanied sometimes with some temporary hormonal turbulence, and that is all it is. In purely physical terms it should be simple to understand, and if necessary, treat. Emotionally however it is rarely so simple, for these events mean different things to each of us inside ourselves, not always fully consciously. Individual, private anxieties are not helped by ignorance and misunderstanding both of ourselves and from those around us. At worst many feel a real terror that meaningful life is past; that floodings and frustrations and flushes and finally that a collapse into instant sexlessness and senility are just around the corner.

Steriliza-tion

For some, hysterectomy is regarded so lightly as to be seen almost as a contraceptive method should their family be complete. One who would choose tubal sterilization were they otherwise healthy may, in the presence of marginally heavy periods or a minor degree of vaginal prolapse, neither in themselves meriting much action, opt for removal and repair as a convenience.

Such, if well counselled, often feel 'a new woman'; 'wish they had been shot of it years ago'; can be quite evangelical about it among their friends. Thus 'hysterectomy for all' can become as fashionable in some circles as 'vasectomy for all' may in others. But there is the same need for caution among the less sure, the more vulnerable, those who hope for magic improvement in sexual or other difficulties, when surgery is not the answer. 'It is not me. It is my uterus' or 'penis' or 'hormones' or whatever, is a more comfortable self-diagnosis for many than 'psychological'. Perhaps this response owes much not only to the inner imperatives of our society to be sensible, but to the parallel fact that to be 'psychological' implies insanity and, worse, such mental problems are untreatable. It is sad that one should still need to distinguish between the two when psychology and psychiatry have come so far. That one does so need to explain, to reassure, is proved to me daily by the fears of many patients who hear the diagnosis of 'psychosomatic' as accusatory, as suggesting they are mad and beyond not only treatment but respect. If public education can counter that view, opening up the idea that unconscious emotions affect and are affected by both mind and body in otherwise sane and healthy people, many may be more open to receive help.

Neither hysterectomy nor the menopause remove the capacity for sexual enthusiasm or orgasm except in terms of what it means individually: unless it is expected to, or felt somehow that it must. Indeed vaginal hysterectomy, in which the uterus is removed through the vagina from below rather than through an abdominal incision, actually gives the surgeon the opportunity to tighten up and repair a vagina which may have become lax, prolapsed or otherwise stretched, in theory thus encouraging sexual contact and sensation.

Nevertheless, this is an area, in my repeated experience, in which once again Masters and Johnson's finding — that the capacity for orgasm rests in stimulating the supports of the clitoris by the thrusting within [4] — is flawed if the woman, her husband or her surgeon accept it as a universal truth. If it is, of course, then we may say confidently that hysterectomy will make no difference to sex. Nor will it for those women whose capacity for orgasm rests in the clitoris or the muscles and tissues of the entrance or anterior vaginal wall alone. I have met many, however, for whom this has not been true, and has caused serious problems. There is no doubt, in my experience, that some women, and their partners, are accustomed to some pressure sensation on the uterus itself, on the cervix, or on its surrounding tissues, particularly the trigone where the bladder neck meets the cervix, as part of their orgasmic experience. This is naturally even more common when the uterus concerned is bulky, enlarged perhaps by fibroids, lying low in the pelvis and thus giving for her and her partner alike the sensation of fullness, a condition more likely to require hysterectomy. I have met several women who at their first eager attempts after surgery were devastated to find that sensation and the ensuing orgasm lost. They then believe it has gone for good. It is vital, I believe, in pre-hysterectomy counselling to inquire about this, thus giving the couple a chance to re-learn and to know that by concentrating on more anterior pressure and outer tissues orgasm is still possible.

I remember two couples in this context. Irene had feared she would feel 'past it'. She had looked at such feelings and discussed them with her husband and they had together agreed to look upon it as a 'new courtship': approaching sex 'for them' at last, with the worries of contraception over. Emotionally they were quite confident and excited at beginning again, 'knowing' that all the necessary equipment remained. But Irene was unaware that the inner sensations so familiar to her in her previously confident sex-life might be different. The first time after recovery, so eagerly planned and anticipated, she felt 'nothing'. In dismay she faked orgasm; hoped it would come right, and didn't want Ian to know lest she had just 'lost the trick'. But until I met her for a routine check-up three years later, she had never been orgasmic since. Ian had sensed this by now, for they knew each other so very well in this once marvellous side of their relationship. He no longer pressed her. They cuddled, enjoyed giving each other mutual orgasm with play, but were sad. The 'real thing' (her words), 'the real total sharing closeness' was gone, she believed, for good.

Irene: the need to re-learn sexual feeling

We discussed together how when it failed the first time it was as though her worst fears, which she had hoped to deny, that 'everything' would be 'taken away', had been self-perpetuating from that first disappointing moment on. Nevertheless it was the work of a moment to show her that pressure on the muscles of the entrance could lead to an equally good if different pressure sensation; that in manoeuvring her own muscles this could be helped; that somewhere inside, if Ian could simply move slowly or even stay quite still for a few moments on penetration she could feel, think, what the 'right spot' might be. Being the pair they were, they needed no more help from me to find their own 'spot' at once. Her repeated failure was, if you like, emotional: a feeling that her worst suspicions were fulfilled.

The need for re-learning was purely a factual misunderstanding. What a waste of three precious years that they
had not been so instructed before the operation.

Ivor: a   Ivor, with an identical story until the first attempt at
different penetration after hysterectomy, found himself crying out to
feeling his already eager but anxious wife: 'My God! It's gone!' It
without a was he who had found the deeper pressure on her heavy
uterus uterus an habitual though unaware part of his pleasure. He
was impotent thereafter until we met. I do not think our
conversation entirely did justice to the bit of him that had
half expected this, to his feeling somewhere within that his
eager sexuality had somehow damaged Ida and led to the
nightmare, as he saw it, of her need for surgery. It was not
rational of course and certainly not literally true, but the
same sense of fearful responsibility that Nick (Chapter 11)
felt after the 'abattoir' of the labour ward caused a very real
unconscious reaction in Ivor too. Ida, in contrast with Irene,
found no orgasm difficulty that first time. She too had been
looking forward to the reassurance that all was still well;
that she was a 'proper' woman still. Thus Ivor's cry of
anguish at such a potentially important moment, that she
had hoped would prove that he found her as good as ever,
led to her finding it extra difficult to cope with the sense
of 'rejection' of the subsequent and continued impotence.

Biddy: no It must be evident by now that above and beyond these
uncon- physical and practical confusions, the involuntary ending
scious of fertility will mean different things in less conscious
regrets emotional terms to some women — and to their menfolk
— than to others. Further, those for whom their capacity
for conception and mothering are a more than usually
important part of their sexual feelings are likely to be more
deeply affected than others as to the symbolic implications
of this loss. This was brought home to me most vividly by
the words of Biddy, who was thoroughly conscious and
even amused by her awareness of this. She was recounting
to me with relish, her blue eyes flashing with the fun of it,
how she had responded to her gynaecologist's advice that
the time for hysterectomy had come.
    Plump, Irish, jolly, Biddy had been a labour ward sister
in the days when this now distinguished gentleman had

been a humble house surgeon. They had remained fond friends through the years, as he had climbed his professional ladder and she had married and revelled in her love-life and four children, so he held no terrors for her. Her periods had become heavier and heavier. 'Too old, too fat, too scatty for the pill', she told me laughing, 'whether I was a Catholic and a heavy smoker or not!' She was on his examination couch, she told me, and 'to be fair to the lad, I was pouring like a pig!' 'Oh, come on now Biddy, ' he had said. 'You of all people should know it's only a useless lump of muscle now. You've had good use of it and it's been nothing but trouble these last few years. What on earth makes you want to hang on to it now?' 'And I told him,' she said to me, bubbling with spirit and amusement, 'I said to him, it may be only a useless lump o' muscle to you mate, but it's me womanhood to me!' She had her operation of course, and thus, spared her chronic anaemia, was the better for it. Nor, insightful as she had been before, did any unconscious regrets interfere with her continued sexual confidence. But in her perception of the meaning of this lump of muscle to many of us, she had a point.

Psychosexual training does not of course obviate the responsibility for competent physical doctoring. Many hormonal imbalances — premenstrual syndrome, and those surrounding the menopause — do of course affect mood and sexual enthusiasm and are in turn affected by them. They may require appropriate chemical adjustment.

Some women may be specially at risk of a 'bad' change *Fear of* if they have inner reasons for fearing ageing. I have done *ageing* some justice to those for whom potential fertility complicates their sense of positive sexuality, but there are others for whom the end of youth itself may need exploration and preparation and overt mourning, as it were, in anticipation, if the change is not to be a change for the worse emotionally and sexually. There is of course no comparable physical change for men, but the sense that lively life is passing, in themselves or in their partners, may cause equal and parallel crises of confidence for some men who are likewise at special emotional risk, not always conscious until this time comes.

Jenny: Jenny was a healthy, lively, intelligent women just past
fear of 50. She loved her three children, now grown and away, and
meno- enjoyed the increased freedom to return to her own hobbies
pausal and interests between the weekend when they flocked back,
madness with their noisy hungry friends, as she put it, 'multiplied'.
She began to find the night sweats of the menopause
'tiresome', interfering with sleep and her sense of attractiveness in bed, but having suffered a minor inflammation
of a leg vein in one of her pregnancies, did not want to
bother with hormone replacement unless it became a 'real
nightmare'. It had not so become, yet, but Jenny was
surprised to find herself suffering waking 'nightmares' of
a different order. She was getting panic attacks when having
to meet strangers; so much so that she was beginning to
fear going out, despite her real pleasure in her new activities
once she arrived. She was afraid, she told me as I took a
Pap smear for hormone estimation, that she would go mad.
Aware that even the most sensible and independent of
patients often reveal their deepest anxiety at this moment
I suggested we should talk further.

Her mother, it emerged, had gone 'round the twist' at
her menopause; she had required inpatient care in a mental
hospital. Jenny, a healthily rebellious teenager at the time,
had 'felt' — she was aware it was not literally true — that
her emerging sexuality and wilfulness had contributed to
her mother's incomprehensible behaviour and illness. She
had felt too that the illness had driven away her husband,
Jenny's father, and not surprisingly, since she was 'a really
angry bitch then, even though we knew she could not help
it'. He had his own problems, Jenny told me. An ambitious
and hard-driving businessman, he had suffered the promo-
tion over him of a young American when their firm was
taken over by some big conglomerate. Further, Jenny said,
he had been a great athlete in his youth, handsome, 'all his
secretaries chasing him and fluttering their eyelashes'. Jenny
could understand well that, while he continued devotedly
to visit his sick wife in hospital, 'It was awful for him — for
us all — when she barely recognized us; only wept and
groused.' Father had taken one of the said secretaries as a
mistress. The worst thing for Jenny was her guilt, for she
had loved her mother, but had sympathy with him in this.

We should not be surprised then that for Jenny it was
not her own menopause but her terrors of it which led to
panic. Airing this was enough for her to move forward,

without replacement therapy but with confidence. Clearly those with a happy secure family life and grandchildren to look forward to are likely to be in better shape than those who have achieved such success as they can or will in other fields. Those who have devoted themselves to the care of others — ageing relatives perhaps who then die, as well as those of us who do so professionally — may also find their unconscious saying 'What about me, then?'

Others at similar risk are those who have not chosen motherhood at all: career girls, lesbians, the mistresses of married men, or simply those who truly never wanted babies. Rationally, they would not have done differently, but the irrational unconscious part that says 'I wonder if . . .' may give them trouble at this time, when it is too late. Obviously those who have wanted and not achieved motherhood, who have lost a child or who have had terminations in the past may feel this even more strongly.

Jessica, a gifted, elegant woman, had cared devotedly for her ailing mother until she died, at about the time when Jessica was approaching the menopause without any physical discomfort. Indeed she was delighted to be 'shot of' her rather heavy periods. She had never wanted children of her own, and consciously 'sublimated' (her word) her maternal instincts in her successful career as a social worker. Jessica was lesbian, and comfortable about it, though no-one but me and her few faithful friends were aware of it. She was sad that she had never been able to confide this to her mother before she died, feeling that she longed for her understanding and blessing but that this would not have been comprehensible to a mother who had long since stopped nagging her about marriage and children. Jessica had indeed had a male lover or two in her youth, and enjoyed them; she was still popular with men and had warm fun friendships with several. But sexually she had long since realized her true attraction. 'You really should try it,' she kidded me early in our meetings. But later, as we knew each other better and I had made such doctor–patient interpretations as freed her from her need to 'flirt' and test me, and me from my discomfort at this behaviour, she was able to describe freely and sensibly what her love-life meant to her.

Jessica: the darker side of homo-sexuality

Yet the menopause — the idea of the 'change' — was very hard for Jessica. We needed to explore together a number

of might-have-beens: children missed, mother's understanding and acceptance of the 'terrible secret' of her
homosexuality. Another fear was that Jessica felt her lover
loved her for her athleticism and physical beauty; that being
younger than Jessica and having loved younger women
before her, she might stray as Jessica aged. The torment of
her fears and jealousy were devastating to Jessica: she, a
gentle, fond woman, was shattered to become aware of such
passions within her. 'My God,' she would say, 'am I going
to turn, after all, into one of those raging bitchy old
dykes?' She did not, of course, but doubts and unease
about the darker side of her homosexuality were raised and
acknowledged. It was not I who referred to such women
in those savage terms. She herself needed to explore the
bit of her which was critical of the 'bitchy dyke' within her
and to face the fear that it might, in old age, 'take her over'.

I referred earlier to the tragedy of women who in their own
emotional crises at this time become weepy, bad-tempered,
unpredictable, and thus risk driving away their men who
are themselves particularly vulnerable to ageing. Others who
are especially vulnerable to these intimations of mortality
are those who have been, or whose partners have been,
youth-oriented in their vision of their own attractiveness and
importance in life. Models, actresses, athletes; the wives of
athletes or flirts or 'rat race' achievers; all these may be more
worried by the prospect of ageing.

There is a dreadful circular problem here for so many
otherwise loving couples. At a time when the woman needs
to feel not just a dear old soul but irresistible, her man feels
the same. She is miserable and temperamental, wondering
what will become of her now her children are gone perhaps,
and she feels it is their turn to be sexy and fertile now. Can
she retrain, become a professional grandmother?

Few can be surgeons or prime ministers. And in her
physical state she barely has the zip for a coffee-morning
or a day's washing. He, too, his job promotions now
unlikely, his sons beating him at games, needs the
reassurance that he still has the young lion in him. He is
dangerously more likely to find it from the young girl at the
office who, incidentally, sees him as an exciting authority
figure and not slumped with his slippers and cocoa over
'Match of the Day'.

Judy had been a devoted wife and mother. Her marriage *Judy: rage*
had become cosy, its sexual expression chummy — she saw *at the end*
her husband as a dear old soul, and he did her. Unusually, *of*
she had coped tolerantly with his infidelity with a few light- *mothering*
hearted young women, seeing it as irrelevant to their
marriage. In a sense it was, for Judy's own sexual enthusiasm had never been great, much tied up with her wish for
children and friendly domesticity. She was tolerant, that is,
until her own mourning and rage to the gods for the end
of her mothering as represented by the menopause coincided with a girlfriend who wanted her husband all to
herself, wanted his children. The sexual life between Judy's
husband and this new girl was, he told Judy, 'out of this
world. Something I never dreamed could be for me'. He
was unable to let it go, feeling painfully that he must leave
Judy for her if she so insisted. I shared much rage and pain
and self-torture with Judy, but sadly when I last heard these
angry agonies, her hatreds towards her husband and the
interloper and, above all, and most uncomfortably, towards
herself for her failures, were dragging on, unresolved, in
bitter legal wrangles about houses and money. Freud's
perception that these symbolize love is repeatedly justified
in my clinical experience.

Sometimes it is the mistresses who find that the menopause can suddenly face them with the futility of their lost
hopes, the waste of their dreams. He is not going to leave
his wife after all. He is not, perhaps, ever to allow them the
children they once dared to hope for. It is a short step then
to feel the loving sexuality, which brought them so far
together and which made their relationship seem to contain
such unique promise, was flawed after all, that he wanted
her only for 'it'; that he withheld his true self; that she was
'used', exploited, betrayed. Such too may need help to
grieve, to mourn, if they are not to waste the rest of their
lives and sexual talents.

The end of a relationship, whether homo- or heterosexual, *Lost*
whether by divorce or desertion, in hurt or in anger or even *relation-*
by mutual consent, almost always requires that bad feelings *ship*
are aired before individuals may begin to regain their sense
of self-value and look positively to their own new future.
I meet some for whom the drifting apart emotionally and
sexually has been mutual and gradual; some who have

become so mutually despair- and hate-ridden that both are merely glad to be shot of the pressures, and are longing to get on with their separate new lives, but it is rare in my experience to find such true equality of relief. Much more often it is that one partner, despite their wish to be 'civilized' and accepting and forgiving, is more hurt or angry or rejected than the other. These feelings, I believe, must be expressed somehow if only in the privacy of our own rooms or hearts, as must the sense of shame and apology for feeling such natural primitive reactions, if they are not to linger on and interfere with overt mourning and recovery. This was movingly conveyed in the film *Kramer versus Kramer*, by the end of which both partners had, by working through much of the torment, begun to rethink for their child, standing back just a little in some kind of calm.

Infidelity, too, is more bearable for some than for others, and again why such special vulnerability in the hurt partner should lead to a total loss of sexual and personal confidence, or to true depression, will vary with any special vulnerability from other experiences, fact or fantasy, of rejection or of the risks of rivalry.

I occasionally meet someone whose sexually failing marriage has apparently been aided by the confidence gained by one or other partner in an affair or in surrogate therapy. Some, it seems, can bring their new-found sexual talents home and share with their partner something of what they now understand that they need. However, in my experience this is so rare that I could never encourage such 'therapy' or partner-swopping and guarantee the marriage would survive it. So much more common, I find, is that if the outside experience is worth doing, it becomes worth continuing. If not, nothing is solved, and the sense of inadequacy reinforced. And if it does work well, the sense of personal inadequacy of the partner left behind is thereby reinforced.

Mary: never a person in her own right   I have met many whose personal confidence is so low that the infidelity or desertion of their partners causes a devastating, even suicidal, sense of rage and loss so intense that, without prolonged and deep supportive therapy, no new beginning is possible. It is as if they feel their very identity has been destroyed. One such — Mary — said to me when we had worked through much of her initial rage and pain: 'It seems I have always thought of myself as somebody's something; never as a person in my own right.' We could see together that she had been first, in her own eyes, a daughter, of powerful, idealized, talented parents: 'their little girl'. Soon then she had become a 'sister', to the heir to the family business — her interloping, for her, younger brother. In retreat from this, or in less than conscious attempt to escape from it, to prove something, she had married young, the first who asked her, not too wisely emotionally, although on the surface she and Mick were a good match. She had thus become 'his wife', and later a 'mother of her children', whom she 'put first', in hindsight, in a compulsive need to avoid repeating the neglect, as she had felt it, of her own parenting. By now she was about to become 'somebody's grandmother'. Long frigid, all her libido being concentrated on her efforts to be a perfect mother, to her horror, Mick, an honourable, devoted and previously faithful man despite their sexual inadequacies, fell for a divorcee neighbour, a long-time friend of both, who wanted him passionately and wanted him 'yesterday'. Mary's need to deny the realities within herself, to be blind to the fact that this could be happening to her, resulted in tormented, irrational misery and bitterness. It was extremely difficult to put her in touch with the long lost part of her that was hers and hers alone; that could move on and live positively without the sense of being 'somebody's something'; that might, indeed, love again herself one day.

Mary's pain and confusion was the greater because she had reached that stage of her life when her mothering role, on which she had depended so deeply for her sense of purpose in life, would have been coming to an end anyway. Her youngest daughter was off to university in the Autumn and for the first time, with or without Mick, she would have found her life empty. Sadly it was, in some sense, her feeling that motherhood was more important than wifehood which had led to their sexual difficulties and to Mick's sense that he was only wanted as a father is the first place. Further, in her anguish, Mary suddenly became demanding, nagging, putting great pressures upon Mick who was tormented enough and guilty enough in himself, shattered as he was by his own sense of surprise and shame that he, a settled family man, should find himself torn by long forgotten passions and sexual revival. Thus, tragically, for given time the affair might have blown over, Mary's confusion merely served to drive him further away. In the arms of his beloved he felt like a lion, and of value as he was — for himself, warts and all. He began to dread returning home, where instead of finding Mary as she had always been — agreeable, uninterested, but at least fond and comfortable — he would find a raging virago: weeping, threatening, illogical, critical. She was, of course, entitled so to feel, but Mick was the more torn and indecisive because he felt he owed her so much. Had she been less vulnerable, calmer perhaps, it might well have resolved itself in time.

I meet so many couples in like situations for whom if the 'offended' partner can stay at least reasonable, later even forgiving, the odds are heavily weighted towards the status quo. To break a long-standing relationship can never be done lightly, however selfish and cynical the 'erring' partner and his or her new mate may like to think they can be. Practical arrangements, money, houses, children, not to mention mere familiarity, weigh heavily against the delights of any new beginning, however much it may seem true love at least for those concerned. Can the original partner but hang in there with some degree of tolerance, it often happens that when the first flush of sexual passion is over, with the reawakened sense of self-value that perhaps only such passion can bring, the 'outsider', understandably, begins to exert pressure. 'When are you going to leave your husband', or 'wife', or 'You promised', or 'You know I want my own children' (to one perhaps already worrying about how he can support his first family). And suddenly the fond old soul at home has won. It is, of course, easy to commend as a cool referee/therapist; not many of us can actually manage it in the torture and fury of the moment, especially as there can be few who are not uncomfortably aware that in some failing or other we have asked for it.

I have told of Mary first because it is perhaps more often the man who strays: often the husband of a sexually unresponsive wife who has devoted her energies towards mothering her children rather than being a lover to her husband. Inevitably, such women get most of the sympathy and perhaps rightly so. We should be cautious, however, if we are prepared to take on equal responsibilities as well as equal rights between the sexes. The often expressed idea, felt often by the men themselves too, thus reinforcing their sense of shame about their need to escape, that 'she has

given him her best years', may for the individual concerned
need cool appraisal. Given? In some ways of course, but
in some ways he has 'given' those years too, be it in the
fruits of his labour or his mere company. If the word 'shared'
were more often used instead, every relationship's value
system might be uncomfortably revealed, but might at least
stand some chance of review. It is wretched for either
partner to feel a door-mat, even for the sake of sympathy.
That frame of mind, of being over-sorry for oneself, lacks
the inner personal sense of dignity with which we hope to
survive and build a future. Moreover it is the more likely
to enhance the apparent charms of the newcomer and in
a positive sense to drive the wanted one further and faster
from us.

Harry was the one on the receiving end of his wife's *Harry:*
infidelity. He became impotent, except on rare occasions, *passivity*
and truly depressed, letting his work slide, losing concen- *in the*
tration, with disastrous effects on a competitive business at *face of*
a time of recession. Early on in their marriage she had *genuine*
strayed once before, briefly, when her eagerness (though *affront*
not, interestingly, her capacity for orgasm) had been greater
than his. He had 'forgiven' her then and again much later
when she was (his words) 'screwing around again', with
his partner in business of all people. As he put it to me
glumly and tearfully, 'I was the last to know'. They were
back together, the affair over, but the marriage and their
lively young family were clearly at risk, as he saw it, 'unless
I can keep her happy sexually'.

We had several conversations in which I was struck by
his passivity in the face of genuine affront. He was able to
accept my observation of this to some extent, freeing him
to express some of his righteous indignation without too
much shame. We found ourselves discussing his life-long
sense of 'second-class citizenship'; that he was not entitled
to say 'boo' to anyone, and that it would cause nothing but
criticism and rejection if he should. He was in difficulty with
a woman who mattered to him, if she evoked negative
feelings in him which he then hastily suppressed. There
were various practical aspects of his life as a second-
generation immigrant which made sense of this: of why,
for example, another man he could not say 'boo' to, let alone
black his eye, was his junior 'upstart' business partner. We

discussed, as I have discussed so often with others, how easy it would be to agree that they had confident murderous feelings towards, say, Adolf Hitler. But it is much harder to acknowledge such feelings toward someone we also love and need.

As usual, Harry had seen his mother as both powerful and hard to satisfy. He had never been sure what would please her, what would invite a 'thick ear', and yet her approval was of course very important to him. Clearly, however, his 'aggressive' attitudes, which might better be called confident self-assertiveness, had been felt by him as trouble-provoking. With a father who gave a model of dealing with her tantrums passively, hiding behind a newspaper and leaving Harry, as he felt it, to bear the brunt, Harry's later lack of potency in more ways than one in the face of an unsatisfied but loved woman fell clearly into place.

Conclusion: the rewards of sexual love

We may remember that to love and be loved is a basic human need, even if harder to detect in some angry women or heedless men than in others! Further, there is no reason why sexual loving of some kind, even if necessarily modified physically by illness or disability, should not continue as long as we live. The 'bright young thing' inside each of us is part of ourselves that we can cherish for ourselves if we dare. Some old people keep it shining to their dying breath, and not by maintaining their golf handicap or painting their faces. Remember Caroline (Chapter 2), who at 76 still 'wanted to be matey'? I remember one woman of 95 who came to lunch not long before she died. Hounded in her time from Russia by those she still called the 'bolsheviks', from Europe by Hitler's anti-Semitism, she was writing books and flying about the world like a kid. Crumpled and frail, she told us of the moonlight over 'St Petersburg', of the balls and the jewels, her eyes sparkling, flirting with those of my young friends who had tried to duck out of this social engagement until she actually arrived. They sat captivated, rugger and rock music forgotten, despite the difference in age and politics. And only recently I was referred a man of 75, retired, a life-long diabetic hypertensive, deaf . . . and totally charming. He complained that though he and his wife made love two or three times a week, 'It was not what it was.' His erection was 'occasionally' not as strong as he would wish. He was anxious about this for his wife was a good deal younger than he — only 69.

In 1975 I was asked to contribute a brief guest column for the International Women's Year series in *The Times*. I said there that women — and the same could be said for men too — tend to see their emotions not as talents which enrich choices, but as shameful weaknesses in our materialist intellectual society. The human being at best, I believe, is not merely an animal which knows but a person who feels and dreams, who strives not only for physical prowess and logical truth, but for the stars.

With technology increasingly influencing and threatening to rule our lives, men and women alike may come to be tempted to deny their emotional talents as weaknesses, to believe that the dreamer within is doomed to disappointment and despair. It is but a short step then to see our vulnerability and our neediness as dangerous in themselves to our survival in a world that pays little tribute to such unmeasurable qualities. To love is itself a dangerous game. The risks are formidable, yet the rewards are beyond price. We dare only what we can dare, and we may need help to dare more, in life as in bed. First we must know what we want; we must know ourselves. Only thus may we be our own person, truly free to make the most of the new world we face and the new choices it may offer us. If we deny that rich heritage which we may call our emotions or our spirit or the questing dreamer within, the world will be a bleaker place.

References

Some of the references given in this section are incomplete due to the unavailability of bibliographical details.

1. Balint, M. (1957) *The Doctors, his patient and the Illness.*
2. Prospectus. Institute of Psychosexual Medicine. Available from 11, Chandos St. London.
3. Masters, V.E. and Johnson, W.H. (1956) *Human sexual response*
4. Masters, V.E. and Johnson, W.H. (1970) *Human Sexual inadequacy*
5. Kaplan, H.S. (1974) *The new Sex Therapy*
6. Friedman, L.J. (1962) *Virgin Wives.* Tavistock
7. Lincoln, R. and Thexton, R. (1979) Preliminary research findings in patients presenting with non-ejaculation *Br. J. Sex. Med* **6**; 55–7
8. Howard, Geraldine (1978) Motivation for vasectomy *Lancet*
9. Howard, Geraldine (1979) The quality of marriage before and after vasectomy *Br. J. Sex Med.*
10. Howard, Geraldine (1982) Who asks for vasectomy reversal and why? *Br. Med. J.*
11. Tobert, A. (1990) Sexual problems in pregnancy and the post-natal period *Midwife Health,* Visitor & Community Nurs. **26** (v 5), 177–80.
12. McIntyre, Sally (1977) *Single and Pregnant.*

13. Blair, M. (1977) Abortion solves only the immediate problem *Modern Medicine*
14. Tunnadine, D. and Green, R.(1978) *Unwanted pregnancy – Accident or illness*

Index